# Cambridge Elements ≡

Elements in New Religious Movements
Series Editor
Rebecca Moore
*San Diego State University*
Founding Editor
†James R. Lewis
*Wuhan University*

# JEHOVAH'S WITNESSES

Jolene Chu
*World Headquarters of Jehovah's Witnesses*
Ollimatti Peltonen
*European Association of Jehovah's Witnesses*

CAMBRIDGE
UNIVERSITY PRESS

Shaftesbury Road, Cambridge CB2 8EA, United Kingdom

One Liberty Plaza, 20th Floor, New York, NY 10006, USA

477 Williamstown Road, Port Melbourne, VIC 3207, Australia

314–321, 3rd Floor, Plot 3, Splendor Forum, Jasola District Centre, New Delhi – 110025, India

103 Penang Road, #05–06/07, Visioncrest Commercial, Singapore 238467

Cambridge University Press is part of Cambridge University Press & Assessment, a department of the University of Cambridge.

We share the University's mission to contribute to society through the pursuit of education, learning and research at the highest international levels of excellence.

www.cambridge.org
Information on this title: www.cambridge.org/9781009509763

DOI: 10.1017/9781009375191

First published 2024

*A catalogue record for this publication is available from the British Library*

ISBN 978-1-009-50976-3 Hardback
ISBN 978-1-009-37518-4 Paperback
ISSN 2635-232X (online)
ISSN 2635-2311 (print)

# Jehovah's Witnesses

## Elements in New Religious Movements

DOI: 10.1017/9781009375191
First published online: November 2024

Jolene Chu
*World Headquarters of Jehovah's Witnesses*
Ollimatti Peltonen
*European Association of Jehovah's Witnesses*
Author for correspondence: Jolene Chu, jochu@jw.org

**Abstract:** Jehovah's Witnesses began as an informal Bible study group in the 1870s that sought to recover first-century Christian beliefs and practices. They disseminated literature announcing the expected reign of God's Kingdom and called themselves Bible Students. In 1931, they adopted the name Jehovah's Witnesses, epitomizing their belief in the Christian obligation to preach the gospel worldwide. Known for their ethic of nonviolence and their evangelizing work, and despite worshipping freely in most countries, Witnesses are subject to controversy, particularly vis-à-vis mainstream Christianity, the State, and secularized societies. The authors are practicing Jehovah's Witnesses who present this work as neither apologia nor official account, but as an emic description of the history, beliefs, identity, and organizational structure of Witnesses, and their societal interactions. While briefly covering main controversies, this Element focuses on the culture and lived experience of the millions comprising the Witness community.

*This title is also available as Open Access on Cambridge Core.*

**Keywords:** Jehovah's Witnesses, International Bible Students Association, freedom of religion, millennialism, law and religion

ISBNs: 9781009509763 (HB), 9781009375184 (PB), 9781009375191 (OC)
ISSNs: 2635-232X (online), 2635-2311 (print)

# Contents

## Foreword

Jehovah's Witnesses are, paradoxically, one of the most widely known at the same time as being one of the least understood of today's minority religions. Commonly recognized as a result of their resolute determination to offer their understanding of God's Truths to every living person, throughout the world, we can see Witnesses standing in rain or sunshine in public places, offering us samples of their literature (which has been translated into well over 1,000 languages, including sign languages), knocking on our front doors, inviting us to discuss our faith in God and, should we engage in conversation, encouraging us to attend a Bible study session. And, despite the fact that only a small minority of those who do undertake further Bible study will become baptized, the Witnesses' persistence has, over the past 150 years, built up a membership of more than 8.8 million in 239 countries. We may also have heard that in present-day Russia the Witnesses have been "liquidated." This is because they openly claim that their beliefs are the true beliefs (although what religions, one may ask, are not of a similar persuasion?) and because their publications (and thus the Witnesses themselves) are officially defined as extremist. Any serious scholar of religion would dismiss this claim as rubbish, yet ironically there is a very different sense in which Witnesses could be viewed as extremist – certainly not in the sense that either jihadi terrorists (as one "extreme") or isolated hermits (as another "extreme") are extremist. On the contrary, Witnesses refuse to take up arms in any circumstances, and, far from living cloistered lives, most live in nuclear families, send their children to "ordinary" schools and have "ordinary" jobs, though these tend to be such as not to interfere with their responsibilities for spreading their truth to the four corners of the world.

In short, it is the seriousness with which Witnesses take their religion that is extreme. They are prepared to go to prison or even die rather than break the sixth commandment, *Thou shalt not kill*. And, although they are in many ways exemplary citizens of whatever state they inhabit, they will obey the law – Caesar's law – only insofar as it does not offend against what they deem to be God's law. Thousands were incarcerated, with about 1,750 dying in Nazi concentration camps during World War II, although, unlike Jews, Roma and homosexuals, whose fate was sealed, Witnesses could have escaped the horrors of Auschwitz simply by complying with the requirement to pledge allegiance to the regime. One reason why Witnesses can exhibit such extreme steadfastness to their principles could well be the belief that after death they will live in a restored Paradise on earth as subjects of God's Kingdom.

While their beliefs and practices clearly form a coherent whole for the Witnesses, some of their actions might seem somewhat surprising to non-believers. Although Witnesses will not vote or lobby for political ends, they have, through numerous legal battles, succeeded in changing or at least clarifying international and national law on a number of issues, mostly related to religious freedoms and human rights. Although Witnesses tend not to encourage higher education for the majority of their members, they have been responsible for supporting those with little access to any education. They have taught more than 152,000 Mexicans to read and write since 1946.

Although Witnesses will not accept blood transfusions, they have contributed to medical progress by facilitating the development of what are sometimes safer alternatives. Although Witnesses understand the Scriptures to be inspired by God and, as such, inerrant, this does not mean that everything in them is taken literally. Although Witnesses who are deemed to have committed serious sins may be "disfellowshipped," a practice that can experienced as resulting in considerable emotional distress, they can be welcomed back into the community if it is accepted that they have truly repented of their wrongdoing. Although they form a close-knit community (referring to each other as brother or sister) and are anxious to protect their members, especially their children, from the influences of the secular world, we are told that nearly half the Witnesses surveyed in Kazakhstan were in an interfaith marriage.

There are a few excellent publications about Jehovah's Witnesses written by social scientists and historians (most of which are referenced in this volume), but almost all those written by individuals who have themselves experienced life in the movement have tended to be exposés by apostates – J. Gordon Melton has identified 138 autobiographical memoirs written by former Witnesses since 2000 (private communication).

Jolene Chu and Ollimatti Peltonen are, however, both fully committed Jehovah's Witnesses who hold academic degrees, and I find it hard to believe that an outsider could have bettered this comprehensive and lucid introduction to an emic understanding of Watch Tower history, beliefs, and practices. Although not all those who read these pages will be tempted to accept the Witnesses' beliefs and lifestyle, we are given a rare opportunity to comprehend more clearly why some of our fellow human beings do accept them – and this cannot but be a good thing.

Eileen Barker

# Introduction

Not so long ago, a manuscript of this kind would have had little chance of seeing the light of day. The prevailing opinion of "insider research" in times past was well captured by intellectual historian David Hollinger, who quipped that "religion is too important to be left in the hands of people who believe in it" (qtd. in Lofton 2020: 1). Unease over inside researcher bias is of course a legitimate concern, in this case, that the authors, both raised in Witness households, would allow their personal sympathies to govern their editorial choices about the content of this work. In full awareness of the challenges of our positionality, we hope to make a meaningful contribution to the small but growing field of scholarship on Jehovah's Witnesses.

Witnesses trace their modern origins to the 1870s and currently number more than 8.8 million in 239 countries and territories. The community's size and its 150-year history raise the question of its inclusion in a series on New Religious Movements (NRMs). Witnesses themselves would reject the NRM label, maintaining that their religion is not new but rather a restoration of early Christian belief and practice. Among scholars, NRM remains a "contested concept" (Chryssides & Whitehead 2023). Some would say Witnesses qualify because they are relatively new; others would say they *were* but no longer are an NRM. Still others classify the religion as an NRM because of its marginal status vis-à-vis the religious establishment. Definitional nuances aside, Witnesses are often buffeted by the same cultural and political headwinds as relatively newer minority religions, which partly explains why academic discourse about Witnesses continues within NRM circles.

Scholarly literature on the Witnesses commonly follows two basic tracks: (1) comparative approaches that highlight, for instance, how the belief system differs from mainstream religion or how the Witnesses navigate their minoritarian positions within wider society; and (2) analyses of controversies and conflicts that trace the roots of debates and examine responses and impacts thereto. These approaches have made important contributions, the majority of which assume a largely etic perspective. Even works that cover the lives of individual Witnesses tend to focus on narrow contexts, such as episodes of religious persecution or other crisis situations. Few works explore the quotidian experiences of ordinary Witnesses, and even fewer studies delve into the cultural and epistemological backdrops of their beliefs and practices. This Element seeks to fill a gap in the literature by offering an emic, or inside, perspective of the worldview of Jehovah's Witnesses on both a collective and an individual level. High-profile controversies and lesser-known accomplishments are discussed briefly; however, the greater proportion of text is devoted to outlining the broader picture of how Jehovah's Witnesses see themselves and take their place in the world.

The history section describes the origin and trajectory of the Witness community up to the mid-twentieth century. The doctrine section outlines the tenets and principles of their belief system, noting major differences with mainstream Christian religions, while avoiding digression into doctrinal disputation. The identity section describes the processes of becoming and belonging, as well as modes of exit and reentry. The section on organization continues from the mid-twentieth century onward with local and global developments that involve virtually all Witnesses in some way. The interaction section covers the Witnesses' relationship with society regarding government, legal and medical issues, and other areas. Finally, the conclusion suggests directions for future research.

Most academic works about Witnesses are geographically bounded. This Element, by contrast, highlights the community's worldwide scope. Statistical data, including recent quantitative research and previously unpublished material, convey the breadth of the community's diversity and collective activities. Witnesses' individual, communal, and organizational perspectives are included – voices largely absent from scholarly discourse to date.

Inclusion of all these essential aspects of Jehovah's Witnesses may leave some readers unsatisfied with sparse treatment of subjects of their particular interest. However, we hope that discussing the interrelationship of major features of the belief system from an emic perspective adds a fruitful vantage point for exploration. We also suggest a number of understudied topics that could be particularly enriched by including insider views as part of comprehensive scholarly analysis.

## Literature Review

In 1997, sociologist of religion Rodney Stark and economics professor Laurence Iannaccone co-authored the article "Why Jehovah's Witnesses Grow *so* Rapidly," describing the group as "one of the most significant religious movements of modern times" (Stark & Iannaccone 1997: 133, italics in original title). Yet, they noted a paradox: "Almost every reader of this essay will have been visited by Jehovah's Witnesses during the past several years. However, if the Witnesses frequently appear on our doorsteps, they are conspicuously absent from our journals" (133). The authors mentioned the "almost complete omission" of the topic from scholarly literature, including the *Journal for the Scientific Study of Religion*, where theirs was the first article on Jehovah's Witnesses in the journal's history. In the quarter century since their article, significant works in sociology, medicine, history, and law have narrowed the gap. But scholarship from the perspective of lived experience is still rare, though recent ethnographies have begun to fill this vacuum. Cross-cultural studies are virtually nonexistent.

The lacunae may be due to several factors. Historians and social scientists have typically approached their work from a strictly secular viewpoint (Lofton 2020; Pohran 2022). Scholars of religion have mainly examined the Witnesses' perceived minority and marginal status. Academic studies lean toward issues unrepresentative of the experience of most Witnesses. Histories often focus on periods of tension with political authority, such as during wartime or under dictatorships. Doctrinal analysis favors those concepts that stoke controversy, with discussion revolving more around disputes and consequences than a given core belief itself – its intellectual origin, its place within the belief system, and perceptions and experiences of believers.

Among other impediments facing scholars, attempts to access the Witness community have sometimes been met with suspicion by potential study subjects who, like other marginal communities, have felt misrepresented by journalists or demeaned by academics (cf. Bromley 2007). Other scholars studying Witnesses up close have recoiled when finding themselves subjected to evangelizing efforts (Holden 2002). Categorization poses another challenge. Though they consider theirs an expression of authentic Christianity, Witnesses are generally classified as neither Catholic nor Protestant – and not even Christian – according to creedal orthodoxy. Statistical data on Witnesses in censuses and surveys often disappear into aggregates with other minorities; or, when reported separately, sample sizes are usually too small for meaningful analysis.

Some scholars analyze Witness beliefs from a broad perspective, framing contested concepts as variations on practices and beliefs common to many religions, such as religious observances, sexual and reproductive issues, medical ethics, ecclesiastical discipline, and family relations (Rigal-Cellard 2020; Introvigne 2024; cf. Hammer & Swartz-Hammer 2024). International tribunals and high courts have similarly ruled that Witnesses are entitled to the same rights as other religions (e.g., *Taganrog LRO and Others v. Russia*).[1] Experts on religious freedom examine the foundational role Witnesses have played in defining, establishing, and expanding the broader collective rights not only of religious minorities but all manner of social groups (Richardson 2017; Knox 2018).

With literature reviews available elsewhere, such as those by Chryssides (2016) and Knox (2017), we instead provide an approximate chronological

---

[1] The 2022 decision by the European Court of Human Rights in *Taganrog LRO and Others v. Russia* (Application no. 32401/10 and 19 others, June 7, 2022 [Final July 9, 2022]) followed this line of reasoning, noting that contested features of the Witness faith can be found in most religions. The Court stated that those who leveled charges of "extremism" provided no concrete evidence of harm. https://hudoc.echr.coe.int/eng?i=001-217535.

periodization of various genres of literature on Jehovah's Witnesses, including works that do not specifically mention Witnesses, but have influenced academic approaches to the subject.

During the 1870s to early 1900s, the nascent community was virtually synonymous with the readership of publications produced by Charles Taze Russell, leading thinker, writer, and founder of Zion's Watch Tower Tract Society[2] and the International Bible Students Association. The group attracted no scholarly attention. The earliest outside writings came from two sources: (1) denominational critiques branding Russell's views as heretical; and (2) former associates of Russell who publicly leveled accusations of doctrinal error, business fraud, and scandalous conduct.

Disputes escalated during the 1910s to 1930s. The widely distributed series *The Fundamentals: A Testimony to the Truth*[3] carried William G. Moorehead's article "Millennial Dawn: A Counterfeit of Christianity" (1910). Denominational criticism increased thereafter, some casting Bible Students as uneducated and gullible victims of a charismatic charlatan (e.g., Haldeman 1915). After Russell's death in October 1916, a succession crisis produced several schismatic groups and a new round of polemical literature. Some theologians combined doctrinal and political lines of attack reflective of wartime conditions (Case 1918). Much vitriol targeted the Watch Tower Society's new president, Joseph F. Rutherford, whose criticisms of mainstream churches sharpened from 1919 onward.[4] During the interwar period, caustic interreligious rhetoric intensified, each castigating the other for having abandoned genuine Christianity.

Two influential works by theologians – Ernst Troeltsch's *The Social Teaching of the Churches* (1931, English translation) and H. Richard Niebuhr's *The Social Sources of Denominationalism* (1929) – utilized sociological concepts to analyze religion in the social terms of class and power relations. According to "deprivation theory," so-called sects appeal primarily to unlettered masses seeking compensation for life's privations. This assertion, mapped onto prevailing negative portrayals of Bible Student leadership, provided a ready explanation for the group's appeal for those described in an early study as "earnest, harmless folk" who were "tactless and ignorant" (Czatt 1933: 22).[5] The concept of social deprivation has a certain explanatory value and aligns with biblical portraits of those drawn to

---

[2]  Zion's Watch Tower Tract Society (founded 1881) was incorporated by the state of Pennsylvania, USA, in 1884. Similar entities have been established, where required, to support the religious activities of Jehovah's Witnesses.

[3]  Regarded as the theological basis for the modern form of fundamentalist Christianity.

[4]  By then renamed Watch Tower Bible and Tract Society.

[5]  Czatt sent out about 500 questionnaires to Bible Students, surveying the leadership of "ministers and laymen." Questionnaire response rates are unstated, but his "fragmentary information"

early Christianity (cf. Tokmantcev 2023; Matthew 5:3–6; 11:28–30). However, positioning deprivation as the primary explanation for the religion's appeal may have contributed to the conspicuous dearth of scholarly accounting for the agency of individual believers (cf. Hickman & Webster, in press).

Sociological research during the 1940s through the 1960s examined the organization's growth and structure. Studies often referenced deprivation theory in describing economic, social, and intellectual deficits or psychological propensities of adherents, and isolated the Witness doctrine of the impending Millennium as the proverbial carrot that attracts the disinherited. Werner Cohn (1955) labeled Jehovah's Witnesses as a "proletarian movement," proposing certain parallels with totalitarian and radical ideologies, including Nazism and Communism. The labels of "authoritarian" and "totalitarian" still appear in scholarly works about Witnesses (e.g., Holden 2002).

Religion/state relations received considerable attention with scholars examining Witnesses' nonviolent stance in Allied and Axis countries, most notably, Nazi Germany. American civil rights experts wrote of Witnesses' court victories that upheld fundamental freedoms of speech and religion (Chaffee 1941). The period of decolonization generated studies such as Norman Long's 1968 sociological analysis that challenged the applicability of deprivation theory to upwardly mobile Zambian Witnesses.

In the 1970s to 1980s, further sociological research probed the affiliation process. Bryan Wilson's studies in Belgium, Japan, and Kenya assessed individual motivations for adopting the Witness faith (Wilson 1973, 1977; Dobbelaere & Wilson 1980). By tracking kinship ties and growth patterns, Wilson argued that the Witnesses do not fit the typology of "cults," which are generally assumed to be single-generation phenomena. Wilson also disputed Cohn's characterization of Witnesses as a "proletarian movement" (Wilson 1973: 145). James Beckford's landmark *Trumpet of Prophecy* (1975) about Witnesses in Britain dismissed the usefulness of deprivation theory and church-sect typologies in analyzing the faith. Self-reports of conversion emphasized rational, cognitive change over narratives of sudden transformation, leading Beckford and others to reject reductionist explanations of Witnesses' religious orientation (e.g., Aguirre & Alston 1980). Although scholars welcomed Beckford's work, Roy Wallis, a student of Bryan Wilson's, wrote: "I get little sense of these members *as people*" (Wallis 1976: 523; italics in original).

Wallis' oft-cited *The Elementary Forms of the New Religious Life* (1984) classified churches, sects, and cults as world-affirming, world-accommodating,

---

indicated that Bible Student ranks contained few college-educated or "professional men." Of fifty letters sent, he received eleven replies, which "contained little except further testimony to their meagre [e]conomic and educational outlook" (20–1).

or world-rejecting. Wallis did not mention Witnesses, but later scholars, drawing on his three-part typology, commonly describe the faith as "world-rejecting." This label has had an outsized influence on stereotypes of the religion as secretive, closed, and antisocial (Di Marzio 2020; Chryssides 2022: 75).

The growing use of donor blood in the 1970s gave rise to a substantial body of medico-legal research on Jehovah's Witnesses who refused transfusions based on their belief in the sanctity of blood. Since then, advancements in patient blood management protocols, development of the bioethical concept of patient autonomy, and growing understanding of risks associated with allogeneic (donor) blood use have reduced but not eliminated controversies regarding Witnesses' abstention from certain blood-based treatments (Beaman 2008; Leahy et al. 2017; Balafas et al. 2023; Olejarczyk & Young 2024).

Although Jehovah's Witnesses were not initially targeted during the "cult wars," later on in the 1990s, they became the subject of official inquiries into "sects" and "cults" in France and Germany (Siewert 2004).[6] George Chryssides, Raffaella Di Marzio, Holly Folk, Massimo Introvigne, Sergey Ivanenko, and James Richardson are among NRM scholars who have written about past and recently resurgent anticult criticisms of Witnesses. NRM scholarship and studies in the field of law and religion often situate the Witnesses in the wider struggle for personal and corporate freedoms, including pivotal rulings by the European Court of Human Rights (Côté & Richardson 2001; Richardson 2020).

Historical monographs on Jehovah's Witnesses in North America and Europe include those by Shawn Francis Peters (2000), Hans Hesse (2001), Detlef Garbe (2008), Gerhard Besier and Katarzyna Stokłosa (2016a, 2016b, 2018, 2021), and Zoe Knox (2018), and works covering the Soviet period by Emily Baran (2014) and Artur Artemyev (2021). Anthropologists and sociologists of religion have begun filling an important gap in understanding the intersection of belief and individual action in what has been called "millenarian moral world-building" (Hickman & Webster, in press).

Recent articles by and about disaffiliated Witnesses assert that the Witnesses' religion includes practices considered coercive and harmful to the mental health of those who exit the community (e.g., Luther 2022). Of this genre, it has been observed that "single case studies of impaired members or ex-members and clinical studies are used to negatively generalize about the groups in questions. Specific beliefs and practices are seldom considered" (Namini & Murken 2009: 562). This literature finds a home in the field of psychology, with its historically ambivalent view of religion in general and its tendency to characterize

---

conversion to NRMs as pathological (Saliba 2007; Pargament & Lomax 2013).[7] Former Witnesses with academic backgrounds, such as historian James A. Penton, have published works critical of Witness doctrine and organization.

Finally, practitioners of the faith have occasionally produced reflexive (insider) scholarship (e.g., How & Brumley 1999; Chu 2015; Perkins 2016; Hu & Murata 2024). Increased openness toward reflexive research and collaborative insider/outsider studies may foster further research of this kind.

In this Element, we aim to navigate the roles of scholars and believers by adhering to academic standards while incorporating insights gained during our personal association with the Witness community. While acknowledging controversies, we mainly present the religion on its own terms, describing the faith as understood by its adherents, their sense of religious identity, and their view of their roles inside and outside the community. We take two basic approaches. First, we discuss doctrines and organizational practices in the context of real-world application. For this reason, certain topics are covered in multiple sections of the text. Second, we describe cultural nuances that may help reduce caricatures and foster further study of individual Witnesses as agents of their own religious lives (cf. Richardson 1985). These explanations are not claims of complete uniformity among congregants, but statements that await further examination by scholars who are not content to rely solely on outside analysis, but are also willing to probe and observe within the faith and among its adherents.

## Notes on Terminology

"Jehovah's Witnesses" refers to the collective community, individuals therein, or their organizational belief and practices beginning in 1931 when the name was adopted. From 1910 until 1931, the community used the official designation "International Bible Students' Association." However, because associated individuals commonly used the term even before 1910, the capitalized designation "Bible Students" is used herein to refer to the faith community from the late nineteenth century until 1931.

"Faith community" refers both to the early Bible Students and Jehovah's Witnesses, depending on the context. Witnesses previously used the term "Society" (or "Watch Tower Society") for organizational matters, whereas the current term is "organization." Regardless of time period, we use the term "organization" for consistency.

Opinions vary on when Jehovah's Witnesses could be called a "denomination." As will be discussed, the legal entity, basic organizational objectives, and core beliefs were already established during the 1880s, and the faith community

---

[7] For views of NRM scholars on ex-member testimony, see Bromley (1998).

adopted a specific name in 1910. However, we use the term "denomination" from the 1920s onward as the community conducted its activities under more centralized leadership.

The Witnesses' principal journal, *The Watchtower Announcing Jehovah's Kingdom*, has changed title several times over its 145-year history. It will mainly be referred to as *The Watchtower.*

Jehovah's Witnesses use various terms to describe their public volunteer work of sharing their beliefs, such as "Bible education," "evangelizing," "preaching," "public ministry," and "witnessing." These terms are used interchangeably herein. Organizational terms related to public outreach include "publisher" (a Witness who evangelizes), "pioneer" (one regularly devoting increased time to evangelizing), and "full-time ministry" (encompassing evangelizing and other forms of volunteer religious activity).

Finally, except where noted, Bible quotations are from the *New World Translation of the Holy Scriptures* (2013), published by Jehovah's Witnesses.

## 1 History

All religions have their unique historical contexts. Exploring the genealogy of a religion's distinctive characteristics can provide insight into its current identities, beliefs, and practices. This section offers an interpretive historical narrative of how Jehovah's Witnesses became who they are today, both doctrinally and organizationally.[8]

To elucidate main aspects of their historical development, this condensed account, as told mainly in contemporary Watch Tower publications, is subdivided into three overlapping themes: their doctrinal origins, early community formation, and evangelizing mission. The section ends with a brief discussion of developments between World War I and World War II. More recent developments are reserved for later sections of this Element.

### Doctrinal Beginnings

Histories of Jehovah's Witnesses often begin with one young man's quest for religious truth. In 1869, in Pittsburgh, Pennsylvania, United States, seventeen-year-old Charles Taze Russell (1852–1916), having already studied and rejected the creeds of different churches, attended a lecture by Second Adventist preacher Jonas Wendell (1815–1873). That meeting motivated young Russell to resume his study of the Bible "with more zeal and care than ever before" (*Watchtower* 1894: 95). Instead of turning to the churches with his theological

---

[8] For additional commentary on the history of Jehovah's Witnesses, see Chryssides (2016) and Knox (2018).

questions, Charles Russell, then about eighteen years old, invited five like-minded associates to begin a systematic study of the Scriptures.

The group Russell started in 1870 used a consistent, structured methodology: They would discuss the doctrines of various Christian denominations one by one, considering relevant scriptures in various Bible translations, along with lexicons, commentaries, and other reference works. After analyzing related scriptures and being satisfied with the harmony of the verses, "they would finally state their conclusion and make a record of it," as if assembling a doctrinal puzzle (Macmillan 1957: 20).

This Bible study class set out to fact-check Christian beliefs in order to return to Christianity's roots, after the manner of thinkers such as Wycliffe, Huss, Zwingli, Luther, Bunyan, Calvin, Wesley, and others long before them (*Watchtower* 1889). Russell later recalled that studying the Bible with these "truth-seekers in Pittsburgh and Allegheny" from 1870 to 1875 "was a time of constant growth in grace and knowledge and love of God and his word" (*Watchtower* 1894: 95). The group made biblical evidence a precondition for acceptance of any teaching and proved ready to distance themselves from church doctrines that they believed contradicted the Scriptures. They did not claim to have invented new doctrines, as Russell explained:

> We found the important doctrine of justification by faith and not by works had been clearly enunciated by Luther. . . ; that divine justice and power and wisdom were carefully guarded . . . by Presbyterians; that Methodists appreciated and extolled the love and sympathy of God; that Adventists held the precious doctrine of the Lord's return; that Baptists amongst other points held the doctrine of baptism symbolically correctly. . . ; that some Universalists had long held vaguely some thoughts respecting "restitution." And so, nearly all denominations gave evidence that their founders had been feeling after truth: but quite evidently the great Adversary had fought against them. (*Watchtower* 1899: 87)

Thus, the Bible Students did not conduct their study in isolation from other streams of Christian thought. (Russell, for example, was raised Presbyterian and then joined a Congregational church.) The group considered the works of scholars and thinkers of their time. Among them were George Storrs (1796–1879) and George W. Stetson (1815–1879), both of whom questioned the doctrine of the inherent immortality of the soul. In 1876, Russell's group began collaborating with Adventist preacher Nelson H. Barbour (1824–1905). While Russell embraced Barbour's emphasis on end-time prophecy and millennialism, they diverged on other doctrinal views; and in 1878, their cooperation ended over Barbour's denial of the substitutionary value of Christ's death to atone for sin (*Watchtower* 1879a).

The Adventist connection and its early impact on the doctrinal interpretations of Bible Students are clearly crucial (Melton 2009; Chryssides 2016). Chryssides argues that Russell and early Bible Students "emerged" from the Second Adventist tradition; however, in Jehovah's Witnesses' current historical interpretation, the Bible Students' separation from the Adventist circle took place before the group started to develop an organizational structure or a more consistent theology. While they acknowledged their "indebtedness" to other denominations, the Bible Students did not consider their views as derivative of any specific religion, such as Adventism (*Watchtower* 1894: 95).[9] They investigated an array of contemporary biblical scholars who believed that the sixteenth-century Reformation had ultimately failed in fully recovering the fundamental doctrines of the church. For Russell and his associates, reformation was not over. Initially, the Bible study group had no intention of forming a distinct religious community. Yet their studies yielded a coherent canon of teachings, and they soon felt compelled to separate themselves from religious systems that they believed had strayed from the gospel.

Though none were scholars of the original languages of the Bible, their research led them to emphasize etymological precision in using English equivalents of Hebrew and Greek expressions. Whether or not they deliberately used distinctive language to distance themselves from mainstream Christianity, several key doctrinal differences developed from their lexical research.

One early keystone concerned the teaching about hellfire, which they deemed contradictory to the nature of divine justice. They compared their findings with those of contemporary writers and concluded that no place exists where lost souls are eternally tormented.[10] Russell penned *What Say the Scriptures about Hell?* (WTBTS-PA 1896), which asserted that the original meaning of the words (Hebrew *sheol* and Greek *hades*), translated thirty-one times in the King James Version as "hell," actually was "pit" or "grave," not a place of fiery torment (9–11). Russell held that the lake of fire and sulfur and similar biblical references symbolized eternal destruction, not conscious torment.

The rejection of the hellfire doctrine corresponded to another conclusion: Humans do not have an immortal soul, separate from the body. By a systematic linguistic analysis of the word "soul" (Hebrew *nephesh*, Greek *psykhe*) in Scripture, they determined that the Bible teaches "not that man *has* a soul, but that man *is* a soul, or being" (*Watchtower* 1903: 106; italics in original). Death

---

[9] While Melton and others place the Bible Students and Jehovah's Witnesses within the Adventist tradition, Russell strongly objected to the Adventist expectation of the fleshly return of Christ and the literal burning of planet Earth (*Watchtower* 1883: 5; Melton 2009: 591, 593–4).

[10] Russell found agreement with Baptist Henry Grew (1781–1862) and Adventist George Storrs (1796–1879), who had published the writings of Aaron Ellis. See *The Intermediate State* (Grew 1855), *Bible vs. Tradition* (Ellis 1853), and *Six Sermons on the Inquiry – Is There Immortality in Sin and Suffering?* (Storrs 1855).

meant not a transition to another form but a cessation of life. The promise in Revelation that "death will be no more, neither will mourning nor outcry nor pain be anymore" foretold the restoration of God's original purpose for humanity to live on earth forever, not just for a few decades before becoming immortal spirits. Despite Adam and Eve's sin that bequeathed death to their offspring, Christ's ransom would effect redemption and resurrection of the dead. His heavenly rule would restore earthly paradise during a literal period of 1,000 years. These findings deeply touched Charles Russell, who had lost three siblings and then his mother in death by the time he was nine years old. The year of his mother's death brought the horrors of the American Civil War. His anguish moved him to question how a just and all-wise God could conceive of predestination and eternal hellfire. Through intense study, he believed he had found the answers.

The study group's research also led them to reject the doctrine of the Trinity as unscriptural, obscuring the nature of God and the whole concept of the sacrifice of Christ as a ransom. God's personal name, Jehovah (YHWH), distinguished him as the Almighty, separate and distinct from his Son, Jesus (*Watchtower* 1882: 2). Rejecting the Trinity meant their doctrine would collide with virtually all Christian denominations. The group articulated these basic doctrinal pillars in the 1880s, and they still constitute the doctrinal foundation of Jehovah's Witnesses down to the present.

The early community also aspired to understand prophetic chronology. Initially, Charles Russell and his associates were indifferent to the question of when the Millennium would begin – that is, the thousand-year reign of Christ. It was Nelson Barbour who convinced Russell in 1876 that humanity had reached a specific era in the fulfillment of God's purposes. From then on, their quest to understand the timetable of Bible prophecies became the focus of their explorations.[11]

Several contemporary researchers believed that 1914 would mark the restoration of the Kingdom of God, based on the prophetic "times" mentioned in the Bible books of Daniel and Revelation.[12] The "seven times" began when the last king of the Davidic line, Zedekiah, was overthrown.[13] They would end when

---

[11] Among beliefs related to chronology, for a time the Bible Students embraced pyramidology, a theory about the Great Pyramid of Giza popular among nineteenth-century Egyptologists (Russell 1891). The Bible Students officially rejected the theory in 1928 on the grounds that God would not use a pagan edifice to reveal his will.

[12] In 1823, John A. Brown calculated the "seven times" of Daniel to be 2,520 years in length and connected them with the Gentile Times of Luke 21:24. In 1844, E. B. Elliott (1793–1875) drew attention to 1914 as a possible date for the end of the "seven times." Joseph Seiss (1823–1904) shared this view. In 1875, Barbour, using chronology compiled by Christopher Bowen, pointed to 1914 as the end of the Gentile Times.

[13] At variance with most historians, Witnesses date the destruction of Jerusalem to 607 BCE based on the prophecy in Jeremiah that the exile would last seventy years (*Watchtower* 2011a; *Watchtower* 2011b).

David's descendant Jesus Christ would begin his rule, not on earth but from heavenly Jerusalem. Russell agreed with these calculations and wrote an article in October 1876 stating that "the seven times will end in A.D. 1914" (Russell 1876: 27). The December 1879 (1879c) and July 1880 (1880b) issues of *The Watchtower* elaborated on this conclusion. In 1889, Russell published further explanations on the "Times of the Gentiles" in *The Time Is at Hand*. The Bible Students embraced this understanding, and during the prewar period, they widely publicized their view of October 1914 as a pivotal date; yet they were not certain what the year would bring. Some thought the year 1914 could mark a "Time of Trouble" resulting in the annihilation of human institutions, and some expected to be "caught up in the clouds" to meet the Lord.

In retrospect, it is instructive to consider their attitude in the run-up to this highly anticipated period. In October 1912, Russell had said: "Should our expectations for October, 1914, not be realized – for years thereafter – this delay would not invalidate God's Great Plan nor our faith therein" (*Watchtower* 1912: 310). Excitement ran high, but the community exhibited no eschatological fervor, nor did they prepare to withdraw into isolation while waiting to be caught up to heaven. After their expectations failed to materialize, there was no large-scale existential crisis within the faith community. There was disappointment, and some indeed left the faith; but the majority carried on their study of prophecies. They believed that the events of 1914, specifically, the start of the Great War, fulfilled the prophecies of the "last days" (e.g., in Matthew 24 and Revelation 12) and concluded that 1914 had marked the beginning of Christ's heavenly rule, but not yet his Millennial Reign over the earth.

## From Doctrinal Separation to an Established Religion

In July 1879, after almost a decade of scriptural research, the Bible study class took a step toward becoming a defined denomination with the publication of *Zion's Watch Tower and Herald of Christ's Presence* (now *The Watchtower*), the trademark by which the Bible Students and Jehovah's Witnesses became known.[14] The new magazine would neither "beg nor petition" for money (*Watchtower* 1879b: 2). Right from the start, it served as an important tool to spread their doctrinal findings to a larger audience, with scriptural discussions written in a down-to-earth style. Another significant publication in defining Bible Student beliefs was *The Divine Plan of the Ages*, penned by Charles Russell in 1886, his first volume in the series *Millennial Dawn* (later known as *Studies in the Scriptures*). Over a thirty-year period, the series reached a printing

---

[14] Charles Russell became founding editor of the journal, which he started shortly after he broke with Nelson Barbour over the doctrine of the ransom.

of more than 9.4 million copies in twenty-one languages and three forms of Braille. To produce and distribute Bible literature, Russell and several others contributed funds to form Zion's Watch Tower Tract Society in 1881. (Russell had accumulated a private fortune through his businesses and investments, much of which he donated to the cause.) The entity was legally incorporated in 1884, with a board of directors and Charles Russell as president.

Watch Tower literature served as a "pulpit" for Bible Student teachings. Mobilizing the printed word led to the creation of a doctrinal identity among those adopting a shared belief system, paving the way to form Bible study classes where *Watchtower* readers could gather. Within one year of the *Watchtower*'s launch, Russell and other representatives from the Pittsburgh class began visiting towns and cities in nearby states. "Our readers are much scattered. . . . Many places they are totally unacquainted with each other, and thus lose the sympathy and comfort which our Father designed should come to them by 'the assembling of themselves together'" (*Watchtower* 1880a: 2). By 1880, about thirty groups of *Watchtower* subscribers met regularly, forming the genesis of Bible Student congregations.

During this period, the Bible Students also held larger gatherings in Pittsburgh, usually in conjunction with the commemoration of the Lord's Evening Meal, or Last Supper, a simple annual event held on the night before Jesus' death (Nisan 14, according to the Jewish calendar). This event drew Bible Students from surrounding areas, growing larger by the year. The first general convention was held in 1893 in Chicago, Illinois (*Watchtower* 1893: 280). Within ten years, conventions were being held with believers on both sides of the Atlantic.

This account of the origins of Jehovah's Witnesses differs from the classic portrayal of cult formation. The community of believers coalesced through a rather modest historical process, there being no mystical leader with special powers to impart enlightenment through divine pronouncements. In this case, biblical literature constituted the catalyst that moved readers to think and reflect on novel ideas backed by rational argumentation, which engendered faith. The growing body of printed treatises comprised a set of teachings. Excitement over their common beliefs and the desire to share them with others led to the development of an organizational structure with further potential for growth. The fact that the community did not adopt a formal name for several decades indicates that Russell intended neither to constitute a new denomination nor to pursue a career as a religious leader (Chryssides 2016).

In 1894, "pilgrims," that is, well-versed traveling ministers, began visiting individual classes to give spiritual instruction and help organize weekly meetings. Pilgrim work consolidated the organizational structure and contributed to the building of the religious identity of the Bible Students as a distinct faith community. In 1889, to accommodate the growth, a large building named the Bible House was constructed in Pittsburgh. The staff were all volunteers, Bible Students who lived and worked in a communal setting provided by the organization. In 1909, the headquarters moved to Brooklyn, New York, to better oversee the expanding international work.

By the early 1900s, the Bible Students had become a definable faith community with a clear organizational structure. The framework for its development as a worldwide religious community was well underway. The use of the term "classes" for collective study groups underlined their self-identification as students of the Bible. As classes grew in size, they were more commonly referred to as "congregations" or "*ekklesias*." In 1910, the International Bible Students Association was established. The designation Bible Student was already part of the everyday language of the community. However, now it became an official name that designated a distinctive identity and epitomized their common goal: to study the Bible progressively and extensively as the core of their faith. The term "association" was neither confrontational nor exclusive, signifying instead a fellowship of like-minded individuals organized into congregations, just as the early Christians had been.

In 1931, some 15,000 Bible Students, assembled in Columbus, Ohio, adopted the name "Jehovah's Witnesses," which was drawn from Isaiah 43:10 where Jehovah calls on the people of Israel to testify to his Godship. Similarly, Christians were to be witnesses of Jehovah, sanctifying his name and character by publicly testifying to Bible truth as they understood it. The name change marked another key moment in their development as a distinct religious community.

## Preaching

From the outset, the group felt compelled to disseminate its findings to the public, seeing the role of a Christian as involving not just belief in Christ but imitation of his example in spreading the gospel. Preaching would be done in public, not simply by sermons delivered from a pulpit. An 1881 *Watchtower* stated concerning the example set by Jesus and the apostles: "Are you preaching? . . . We were not called, nor anointed to receive honor and amass wealth, but to spend and be spent, and to preach the good news" (*Watchtower* 1881: 2). The Bible Students publicized their beliefs by means of millions of printed pages, most of it distributed without charge. For instance, in one six-month period, about 1.4 million free copies of the 1881 treatise *Food for Thinking Christians: Why Evil Was Permitted and Kindred Topics* were distributed in the United

States and Britain. *Watchtower* subscribers, who numbered perhaps a few thousand in the 1890s, participated in the expansion of their fellowship by distributing free tracts and sample *Watchtowers*. In 1892, more than a half million samples went out, in addition to over 70,000 *Watchtowers* sent free to those on the "poor list" who could not afford the 50-cent subscription fee.

In 1891, Russell led a trip to Europe and the Middle East, the first of several cultural excursions to understand how to meet the spiritual needs of diverse peoples worldwide. By the early 1900s, individuals in numerous countries had embraced Bible Student doctrines from literature translated into vernacular languages. In 1914, the literature was published in more than 30 languages, and about 5,000 Bible Students were evangelizing in over 40 lands.

The Bible Students constantly sought new methods to distribute literature to larger audiences, allowing the community to exert far more influence on the religious scene than its actual size would suggest. Russell's syndicated sermons appeared in a peak of about 2,000 newspapers, reaching millions of readers. In 1914, the Bible Students released the landmark eight-hour colorized film, lantern slide, and synchronized sound presentation *Photo-Drama of Creation*. Recounting history from biblical to modern times, *Photo-Drama* defended the Bible as being the scientifically sound inspired Word of God. The production, shown free to nine million viewers in North America, Europe, and Australia, challenged the theory of evolution and higher criticism of the Bible, ideas the Bible Students considered corrosive to Christian faith (Barnes & Cherchi-Usai, forthcoming).

Expectations for the year 1914 and the impending reign of Christ's Kingdom were central themes of the Bible Students' message during the prewar years. The Bible Students publicized their conclusions so widely that shortly after the Great War erupted, the New York newspaper *The World* stated in the article "End of All Kingdoms in 1914":

> For a quarter of a century past, through preachers and through press, the "International Bible Students" . . . have been proclaiming to the world that the Day of Wrath prophesied in the Bible would dawn in 1914. (*World* 1914: 4, 17)

While pursuing their mission during these decades, the Bible Students experienced considerable growing pains. Besides facing sustained hostility from clerical circles, dissension arose within the fellowship among former associates of Russell and even his own wife, Maria, who separated from him and sued for "divorce of bed and board" (*Watchtower* 1906: 221; Chryssides 2016: 65–8).[15] Disappointment over unfulfilled expectations in 1914 coincided with the outbreak of World War I, overtaking hopes for immediate deliverance. The unexpected

---

[15] The court proceedings were highly publicized and included unsubstantiated allegations of impropriety against Russell that were ultimately stricken from court records.

death of Charles Russell in October 1916 further amplified confusion among some over the Bible Students' organizational identity. Joseph F. Rutherford (1869–1942), successor to Russell as Watch Tower Society president, faced stiff opposition from certain quarters, with some prominent "pilgrims" contesting the centrality of the preaching work to the organization's mission. In 1917, Rutherford dismissed four opposing members of the board of directors who unsuccessfully attempted to take control of the Watch Tower Society, resulting in schismatic groups that rejected the legitimacy of the new presidency (Melton 2009; Chryssides 2016).[16] Rough estimates indicate that Bible Student evangelizers decreased by about 20 percent between 1914 and 1918. The turbulence of the year 1917 would be surpassed, however, by events of the following year.

## Between the World Wars: Consolidating Identity

With the United States fully engaged in the Great War and war hysteria spreading, on May 7, 1918, eight leading Bible Students, including Joseph Rutherford, were arrested for "unlawfully, feloniously and willfully causing insubordination, disloyalty and refusal of duty in the military and naval forces of the United States" (*Watchtower* 1918: 171). A federal court convicted the eight men of conspiracy to violate the Espionage Act and handed them four concurrent sentences of 10–20 years each. Evidence against the defendants primarily revolved around one book, the last volume of the *Studies in the Scriptures* series – *The Finished Mystery* – published in 1917.[17] The book roundly criticized Christian clergy for playing a direct role in fomenting the war. In the months preceding the trial, certain mainstream clergy had publicly accused the apolitical Bible Students of treason (Case 1918). At the sentencing hearing, the judge characterized *The Finished Mystery* as "religious propaganda . . . more harmful than a division of German soldiers" (*Washington Post* 1918: 3; Macmillan 1957: 99).

This bleak moment seemed to deal a death blow to the Bible Students. After the trial, Bible Students throughout the United States suffered mob violence, raids on meeting places, book burnings, imprisonment, and sustained vilification from the press and pulpit (Abrams 1969). The headquarters moved temporarily back to Pittsburgh, and the preaching work remained low key. However, publication of *The Watchtower* continued. In January 1919, in a show of

---

[16] See the *Watchtower* (1917: 327–30) regarding the legal basis for the dismissals. See also *Jehovah's Witnesses in the Divine Purpose* (WTBTS-PA 1959: 70–3) and *Jehovah's Witnesses Proclaimers of God's Kingdom* (WTBTS-PA 1993: 64–8).

[17] Macmillan describes the book as "a compilation of material from notes and writings of Russell" (1957: 80).

support, Watch Tower Society shareholders reelected the prisoners to the board of directors in absentia, and Rutherford retained his position as president.

Less than one year later, the war had ended and war hysteria ebbed. After twice denying them bail pending appeal, the court finally released the eight men on bail in March 1919 and completely exonerated them the following year.[18] This marked a decisive moment in the history of Jehovah's Witnesses. The Bible Students could again freely carry on their ministry; the organizational structure remained intact; and the external and internal struggles subsided.

In September 1919, in Cedar Point, Ohio, the Bible Students held a major convention that underlined the responsibility of each Christian to preach the Word. A 1919 printers' strike in New York City prompted the setup of their own printing plant, which could produce literature much more economically than commercial printers. In-house printing of *The Watchtower* began with the February 1, 1920, issue. A landmark 1922 convention in Cedar Point, Ohio, further emphasized advertising the Kingdom as humanity's only hope. Thereafter, house-to-house visitation became a regular feature of the Bible Students' ministry. They leveraged the relatively new technology of radio networks to reach millions of listeners in North America and Europe.

As the reach of the Bible Students' message spread, so did continued tensions with mainstream clergy. The Bible Students' sharp warnings about the dangers of politicized religion focused on the clergy's role in promoting the recent war, and the perception that religious opponents had been behind the imprisonment of leading Bible Students. In the 1930s, after clergy-led opposition prompted the cancellation of radio broadcasts, evangelizing was done with portable gramophones carried door to door to play short recorded lectures by Rutherford and others (Weiner 2014).[19] The intensified preaching activity differentiated Jehovah's Witnesses even further from mainstream religions, and their high-profile evangelizing in some localities occasionally stirred animosity and physical attacks, usually initiated by local clergymen. Although historical accounts note the Witnesses' confrontational manner in delivering their message, little research has explored the role of Catholic and Protestant clergy in mobilizing popular sentiment and government authority in efforts to suppress the activities of the Witnesses (Peters 2000; Garbe 2008). In the United States, Canada, France, Australia, Germany, and many other countries where

---

[18] On May 5, 1920, the eight men were exonerated when, in open court, the government's attorney announced withdrawal of the prosecution on order of the United States Attorney General.

[19] *Radio Broadcasting, Hearings before the Committee on Merchant Marine, Radio, and Fisheries,* Seventy-Third Congress, Second Session on H.R. 7986 (1934). https://books.google.com/books/about/Radio_Broadcasting.html?id=SB9MjsgQ85UC.

the Bible Students conducted public preaching campaigns, local clergy insti-
gated government opposition, popular riots, police brutality, or mob violence.

The events of the interwar period contributed immensely to the historical
legacy of Jehovah's Witnesses and retain great significance in their religious
narrative. In the 1920s, the Bible Students began to implement a clearly defined
strategy to advertise the gospel worldwide. The core teachings they embraced in
the 1870s and 1880s continued as their foundation, a kind of doctrinal "consti-
tution." However, their examinations of Scripture continued. Now, the Bible
Students became more sensitive to religious practices, scrutinizing the historical
roots of religious customs and traditions, such as Christmas and Easter, and
abandoning those practices deemed pagan in origin. Another important concep-
tual development related to their view of the Kingdom of God as an actual
heavenly government. Consistent with the belief that God's Kingdom had been
ruling since 1914 above all other "kingdoms," or governments, the Bible
Students maintained that Christians should not compromise their loyalty to
the Kingdom by getting involved in politics or supporting the supremacy of
any political ideology. The 1925 *Watchtower* article "Birth of the Nation" urged
separation from the "world," not meaning from surrounding society but from
the world's political, ecclesiastical, and exploitative financial systems that had
by their actions repudiated God's Kingdom (*Watchtower* 1925: 68). The new
name, Jehovah's Witnesses, adopted in 1931, crystallized their identity and their
resolve as an organization to carry the gospel worldwide as a core element of
their Christian faith.

In January 1942, Joseph F. Rutherford died and Nathan H. Knorr (1905–1977)
became the third president of the Watch Tower Society. Knorr, a proficient
organizer, launched an era of education and training with an eye toward global
expansion. This period will be covered in the section on organization.

## 2 Doctrine

This overview of Jehovah's Witnesses' belief system focuses on teachings that
impact the Witnesses' individual and collective worldview. We define the faith's
epistemological boundaries and describe how doctrines connect with one
another and apply in modern life. This section focuses on the beliefs of
Jehovah's Witnesses, rather than all Christian dogmas. Therefore, teachings
are stated in the declarative voice without the qualifying "Jehovah's Witnesses
believe." Key biblical verses and references to Witness literature are included.
We describe communal values and standards of conduct as taught, while
acknowledging that individual levels of conviction, commitment, and compliance vary.

## God, the Bible, and Revealed Truth

The keystone of Jehovah's Witnesses' faith is the belief that the Creator of the universe, Jehovah, exists. He is the Almighty God who seeks to have a fatherly relationship with his intelligent creation.[20] Humans can learn about him from two God-given sources: natural creation and the Bible. Whereas creation powerfully speaks of God's "invisible qualities" (Romans 1:20), the primary way to know God is through the Scriptures.

The truth about God is expressed in the Bible's opening words: "In the beginning, God created the heavens and the earth" (Genesis 1:1). As the Creator, God is the Universal Sovereign, who established the laws governing the natural world. Jehovah, the name God gave himself, is represented by the Hebrew letters YHWH. Derived from a Hebrew verb, this name, understood to mean "He Causes to Become," refers to his supreme ability to create and to fulfill his purposes (*NWT* 2013: 1731, 1735).

Jesus was Jehovah's first creative act – a perfect spirit creature called the "only-begotten Son" and "the beginning of the creation," whom Jehovah used in creating everything else (John 3:16; Revelation 3:14). Witnesses acknowledge that certain Bible verses refer to Jesus' divine, or godlike, nature, but they reject the Trinitarian concept of Jesus as God, or part of a Godhead. They maintain that Jesus held to the monotheistic doctrine of the Jews, never claiming equality with God, let alone declaring himself to be God. Jesus' subordination to God is shown in his various roles, foremost as the Son of God. In contrast to other Christian denominations, Witness doctrine holds that Jesus served as the archangel Michael and as the Word in his prehuman existence – the chief angelic representative who conveyed communications on God's behalf. Jesus came to earth to atone for sin and rescue humans from death and was named Jesus ("Jehovah Is Salvation") at birth, foreshadowing his role as Redeemer. After his baptism by complete immersion, Jesus was anointed by God's holy spirit, thus becoming the Christ, or Messiah, (Anointed One) through whom Jehovah would fulfill his purposes toward humanity. After his death and resurrection, Jesus returned to heaven in spirit form, henceforth immortal but still subject to his Father and Creator.

Holy spirit is not a person but God's invisible energizing force that he used to create, perform miracles, and inspire ancient prophets and Bible writers.[21] Empowered by holy spirit, certain humans in biblical times received miraculous

---

[20] God is referred to as "he," following the gendered pronouns in the original languages of the Bible.

[21] Since the Witnesses see holy spirit as an impersonal force and not the second person of the Trinity, they refer to holy spirit in lower case.

abilities to perform healings and speak foreign languages. Transmission of these "gifts of the spirit" ceased with the death of Jesus' apostles. Jehovah's Witnesses do not practice faith healing, speaking in tongues, or exorcism. However, they believe that holy spirit continues to empower believers to understand the Scriptures, manifest godly qualities, make sound decisions, and withstand tests of their faith.

Jehovah's Witnesses believe that God inspired the writing of the Bible – a canon of 66 books produced by some 40 writers over 1,600 years. Jehovah reveals himself and his purposes through the Bible, which is inerrant and contains both literal and symbolic passages.[22] Although Witness literature often references commentaries, lexicons, Bible encyclopedias, and other religious and secular works, no other source – including Witness publications – approaches the authority of the Bible. The Bible text, as transmitted down through the ages, is reliable. It is internally harmonious, seeming contradictions being due to incomplete or erroneous understanding. All scriptural teachings are consistent with God's personal qualities, the foremost of which is love. The Bible is applicable across nationalities, ethnicities, and cultures, is historically and scientifically accurate, and is a source of reliable prophecy. Although the Mosaic Law, recorded in the Hebrew Scriptures (the preferred term for the Old Testament), is not considered binding on Christians, the principles found there reveal divine views on justice, morals, and other matters, providing insight for those seeking to apply Bible standards in life. The Christian Greek Scriptures (New Testament) chronicle the life and teachings of Jesus and the formative years of Christianity, furnishing a pattern for authentic Christian practice.

Witnesses do not claim to understand every Bible verse. However, because God inspired the Scriptures to reveal himself to humanity, Witness beliefs contain little that could be considered a mystery. Prophecies and "sacred secrets" are divine truths, the meaning of which God would uncover in time (Daniel 12:4; Acts 1:7–8; Romans 16:25–26).

## Modern Religious Authority

Jehovah's Witnesses believe that Jesus laid the foundations for the Christian congregation, which was established after Jesus' death, at Pentecost, in the year 33 CE. A council of apostles and elders in Jerusalem oversaw this community of believers. Holy spirit directed this governing council as it made decisions based on prayer and study of the Hebrew Scriptures. The council dispatched representatives and evangelizers, ruled on doctrinal and moral matters, administered

---

[22] In view of this, Jehovah's Witnesses do not fall into the category of fundamentalists (Chryssides 2022: 43).

material relief, and issued authoritative decrees for observance by Christian congregations (Acts 15; 16:4–5). Yet that structure did not constitute a clergy-laity distinction (Matthew 23:8).

Following this precedent, the Governing Body of Jehovah's Witnesses is composed of men (numbering eleven at the time of printing) who provide religious direction and guidance to the worldwide Witness community. The Governing Body serves as the "faithful and discreet slave," which Jesus described in his prophecy about the last days. The master (Jesus) would appoint the composite slave to provide to fellow slaves "their [spiritual] food at the proper time" (Matthew 24:45–47).[23] The modern-day Governing Body takes the lead in producing this spiritual food – Bible-based publications and study tools – and contributes to the development of Witness doctrine. There are no equivalent positions to the prophets of old or any claim of modern special revelation. The Governing Body's main method of exegesis is the same as the early Bible Students – to "compare scripture with scripture" (*Watchtower* 2006: 12). The Governing Body determines doctrinal understanding through deep, comparative study of Bible texts, prayer, and their perception of the leading of God's holy spirit, similar to biblical descriptions of first-century proceedings.

Witnesses believe that God progressively leads the faithful to accurate doctrinal understanding. The *Watchtower* magazine is the main channel of instruction, containing authoritative statements of doctrine and practice insofar as they are presently understood.[24] The *Watchtower* article "Who Is Leading God's People Today?" states: "The Governing Body is neither inspired nor infallible. Therefore, it can err in doctrinal matters or in organizational direction" (*Watchtower* 2017a: 26). This admission of fallibility is neither surprising nor destabilizing to Witnesses in general.

Especially regarding end-time prophecies, some scholars point to "failed prophecy," citing Witnesses' unfulfilled expectations concerning the year 1975.[25] From an emic perspective, however, even if explanations of biblical prophecy fall short, Witnesses view the prophecy itself as unfailing (Chryssides 2016: 223–43). Just as God led his ancient worshipers incrementally to

---

[23] A major adjustment regarding this designation is discussed in the articles "Feeding Many Through the Hands of a Few" and "Who Really Is the Faithful and Discreet Slave?" (*Watchtower* 2013a: 15–19; *Watchtower* 2013b: 20–5).

[24] *The Watchtower* covers history, prophecy, scriptural ethics, personal improvement, interpersonal relationships, Bible character studies, word studies, and so on. Other study tools include the two-volume Bible encyclopedia *Insight on the Scriptures* and the annotated Study Edition of the *New World Translation of the Holy Scriptures*.

[25] After 1975, Witness numbers dipped temporarily, but no large-scale decrease followed. See *Watchtower* 1975a: 579–81; *Watchtower* 1976: 440–1; and *Watchtower* 1980: 17–18. Stark and Iannaccone (1997) analyzed Witnesses' rates of growth, decline, and recovery in the 1970s and 1980s (142–4).

understand his unfolding purposes, modern-day believers can expect course corrections over time (cf. Daniel 12:8; Acts 1:6–8). Jesus indicated that some prophecies would be understood only during or after fulfillment, stating: "When you see . . . , know" (Matthew 24: 32–34). Therefore, Witnesses do not view their interpretations of Bible prophecies as infallible. Perhaps for this reason, as was the case in 1914, subsequent unfulfilled end-time expectations have not caused an existential crisis in the faith community. Witnesses consider it proper to read current events through the lens of prophecy to discern, not the day and hour, but the general period to expect the fulfillment of prophecies according to God's timetable.

Similarly, Witnesses commonly refer to their belief system as "the truth" even while expecting refinements over time. Emerging social and political issues, revolutionary medical treatments, technological advances, and changing organizational and congregational needs call for clarification on how to apply biblical principles to new situations. Explanations of doctrinal adjustments usually appear in *The Watchtower* or other study publications. More recently, the Governing Body has communicated these adjustments through their regular updates on jw.org. Significant doctrinal changes from 1870 forward are listed by year in the *Watch Tower Publications Index* under the heading "Beliefs Clarified." Despite such occasional adjustments, scholars have described Witness doctrine as "rational" and "relatively unchanging and outstandingly coherent" over time (Beckford 1975: 119; Wilson 1977: 100).

## Views of Other Christian Denominations

The Christian Greek Scriptures prophesied that soon after the death of Jesus and the apostles, apostasy would infiltrate the congregation (Acts 20:29–30; 2 Peter 2:1–2; Jude 3–4). The nascent Christian community faced serious threats to its doctrinal integrity and communal harmony – Jewish attacks on it as heretical; schismatic movements from within; infiltration of Greek philosophy; and challenges to apostolic authority. According to the Witnesses, the writings of the second-century Apostolic Fathers and Apologists already bore early marks of the foretold apostasy, leading to the adoption of Trinitarian doctrine in the fourth century, among other deviations from original Christian thought (2 Thessalonians 2:3–12; *Watchtower* 2009b; *Watchtower* 2010b). Despite broad acceptance of the Trinity among Christian denominations, Witnesses reject the teaching as unscriptural. They maintain that the Trinity's roots in Platonic philosophy, as well as the political currents behind the fourth-century church councils that adopted it, mark it as human philosophy, not divine revelation (WTBTS-PA 1989b: 8–11). Therefore, the doctrine obscures God's nature, making him mysterious and unapproachable. Also, the doctrines of hellfire and predestination are rejected by Witnesses as extrabiblical, likewise misrepresenting God's character and alienating humans from him. Witnesses reject what they consider to be syncretistic doctrines, along with symbols and rituals that many Christian denominations have adopted and deem Christianized, including the cross and Christmas. Witnesses avoid such traditions unless they find a comparable scriptural precedent.

The harlot of Revelation named "Babylon the Great" rides atop a seven-headed wild beast (Revelation 17). Witnesses identify Babylon the Great as the world empire of false religion, which attempts to dominate the beast, the human political system. They especially fault Christian churches throughout history that have been deeply involved in politics and wars. In the Witnesses' view, alliances that religions have made with political powers are acts of disrespect and disloyalty to God and his Kingdom. Avoidance of political involvement partly explains why Jehovah's Witnesses do not promote ecumenism.

## From Rebellion to Redemption

A main theme of the Bible is the ultimate fulfillment of God's purpose for humanity by means of his Kingdom, a heavenly government ruled by Christ Jesus. After creating Jesus, God made other perfect angelic sons, who observed the making of the physical universe over eons of time. During creative "days" of undetermined length (not 24 hours long), God created all life forms on earth. Humans are made in God's image in the sense that their intellectual, moral, and spiritual capacities are of a higher order than animal creation. The human family descended from the first couple, Adam and Eve. Genesis describes God's creation of Adam from the "dust," or elements of the soil, after which Jehovah animated Adam's perfect body with "the breath of life, and the man became a living person" (or "soul") (Genesis 2:7).[26]

The first couple were commanded to procreate and have stewardship over the earth and animal creation; they were prohibited from eating from the tree of the knowledge of good and evil under penalty of death, the tree symbolizing God's authority to define right and wrong. With these commands, the Creator sensitized humans to their moral capacity to know and respect divine standards. Adam and Eve and their offspring would fill the earth. Universal peace would depend on recognition of God's position as Sovereign. Jehovah endowed both

---

[26] Quotation marks for scriptural citations from the *New World Translation* (NWT), published by Jehovah's Witnesses, allow readers to compare NWT renderings with other translations. The NWT has been criticized for its inclusion of the name Jehovah and rendering of verses commonly cited in support of the Trinity doctrine. See further discussion in Section 4 on organization.

intelligent spirit and human creation with free moral agency and clearly defined choices: endless, perfect life for obedience; or eternal death, or nonexistence, for disobedience.

An angel committed the first sin (in Hebrew, "miss the mark," or fall from perfection) by accusing God of imposing unreasonable restrictions on intelligent creation (Revelation 12). Speaking through a serpent, he tempted Eve to eat the forbidden fruit, stating: "You certainly will not die. For God knows that in the very day you eat from it, your eyes will be opened and you will be like God, knowing good and bad" (Genesis 3:1–5). By accusing Jehovah of lying, the angelic rebel defamed God's holy name. The challenger did not claim to be more powerful than God, an issue Jehovah could easily have settled by destroying the rebels. Rather, he claimed God's rulership to be unduly restrictive, thereby justifying moral self-determination and independence from God. This once-perfect angel thus earned the titles Satan ("Adversary") and Devil ("Slanderer").

In the book of Job, Satan further denigrated Jehovah's sovereignty when he derisively questioned Job's integrity, claiming that the wealthy man worshipped God out of selfishness. With God's permission, Satan afflicted Job with suffering and loss, predicting that he would "curse" God to his "very face" (Job 1:11). Satan extended his cynical accusation, claiming: "Skin for skin. A man will give everything that he has for his life" (Job 2:4). In effect, Satan declared that he could turn all humans away from Jehovah.

The accounts of Genesis and Job shed light on the age-old question of theodicy – God's permission of evil – by presenting suffering and evil as temporary conditions arising from Satan's rebellion and humans' claim for independence from God. Before the Edenic rebellion, human suffering and death did not exist (Romans 5:12). Upon rejecting God's sovereignty, Adam and Eve experienced not only moral but physical corruption – they died and returned "to dust." Sin and death passed genetically to Adam's descendants so that even those wishing to live righteously proved unable to free themselves from the effects of inherited sin. The Bible metaphorically speaks of sin as a harsh "king" who pays the "wages" of death to Adam's sinful offspring. As a result, the "soul" (literally, "breather") that sinned would die (Ezekiel 18:4).[27]

Death is compared to unconsciousness or a sleep from which a person can awaken if resurrected (Ecclesiastes 9:5, 10; John 11:11–16). Death is also termed the "last enemy" that opposes the fulfillment of God's original purpose for humankind (1 Corinthians 15:26). Most religions embrace the concept of an immortal spirit or soul that is distinct from the body and survives at death.

---

[27] See *Insight*, "Soul" (WTBTS-PA 2018b: Vol. 2, 1004–7).

However, if all humans have a separate component that survives the body after death, it would mean that all – good and evil – would have immortality. Witnesses maintain that this concept contradicts Jehovah's warning that the penalty for sin is death.

God did not plan – or predestine – the disastrous outcome of sin and death for humanity. Despite his ability to foreordain future events, Jehovah does not determine in advance the course and destiny of each individual.[28] Witnesses believe that predetermining every act and the destiny of every human would be inconsistent with God's qualities of love and justice and would contradict scriptures that indicate that humans have freedom of choice (e.g., Deuteronomy 30:19–20).

Before expelling Adam and Eve from Eden, Jehovah decreed that the serpent would finally be crushed by an opponent, an "offspring." (Genesis 3:15). This promise to eliminate Satan confirmed that God's original purpose for humankind would yet reach fulfillment. To this end, Jehovah God has concluded a series of covenants, or formal agreements, throughout biblical history that progressively established a legal basis for humanity's redemption. These covenants also revealed the lineage of the foretold offspring – the Messiah who would crush the serpent (Satan) and liberate humans from Satanic domination.

God's covenant with Abraham promised that through his offspring, "all nations of the earth will obtain a blessing" (Genesis 22:18). The family line would pass through Abraham and Sarah's grandson Jacob (renamed Israel) and the nation he fathered. At Mount Sinai, Jehovah concluded the Law covenant with the nation of Israel, including its arrangement of sacrifices to atone for sin. God then promised Israelite King David that his throne would be "established forever" through his offspring (2 Samuel 7:16). The line of Davidic kings was interrupted when the Babylonians deposed Zedekiah and destroyed Jerusalem and its temple. About six centuries later, God transferred the life of his perfect spirit son from heaven to the womb of the Jewish virgin Mary to be born as a human. Jesus, untainted by Adamic sin and born in David's family line, would be that promised offspring and the king whose rule would restore Paradise to the earth.

Jesus perfectly mirrored God's qualities and displayed prayerful obedience to his Father's will (Hebrews 5:7–8). Jesus directed all glory for his miracles to his Father (John 7:16–18; 11:41; 17:4). He became known as the masterful teacher of the good news of the Kingdom, the heavenly government that he would one day rule. Jesus has always been and always will be subordinate to God, as his title Christ denotes. His life on earth demonstrated that a perfect human,

---

[28] See *Insight*, "Foreknowledge, Foreordination" (WTBTS-PA 2018a: Vol. 1, 851–60).

motivated by love for God, could maintain flawless integrity despite undergoing temptation and brutal execution on a torture stake (1 Peter 2:21–22; 1 John 5:3).

The night before he died, Jesus instituted the Lord's Evening Meal, a yearly commemoration of his sacrificial death as the lamb of God who would provide permanent atonement for sin.[29] By presenting his own perfect life as a substitutionary ransom, he bought back the opportunity for eternal life for Adam's descendants, releasing them from the curse of inherited sin and death.

Jesus told his disciples that after his death and resurrection, he would return to the glory he had "alongside [his Father] before the world was," where he would prepare a place for them (John 14:2–3; 17:5). He introduced the "new covenant" (replacing the Law covenant) and the Kingdom covenant so that his apostles could serve as co-rulers in his heavenly Kingdom (Luke 12:32; 22:28–30). Recalling God's promise to Abraham, the book of Galatians states that Jews and non-Jews, males and females, slaves and free persons would become part of Abraham's offspring and "the Israel of God" (Galatians 3:26–29; 6:16). These would be "born again," anointed by God's holy spirit, adopted as "God's children," and granted immortality as spirit beings in heaven (John 3:3–8; Romans 8:14–17). From the first century CE until now, God has been selecting Christian men and women to be part of the 144,000 who will rule with Christ in heaven during the Millennium (Revelation 5:10; 7:4; 14:1–3; 2 Corinthians 1:21–22). While still on earth, anointed ones today abide by the teachings and congregational arrangements common to all Jehovah's Witnesses.[30]

Unlike the mainstream religious concept of heaven as the destination for the saved upon death, Witnesses believe that the majority of saved humanity will live in a restored Paradise on earth as subjects of God's Kingdom (*Watchtower* 2009a: 8; *Watchtower* 2016: 21).

Jesus' miraculous acts and his care of the poor and oppressed foreshadowed the blessings of his millennial rule. As "the resurrection and the life," he has been empowered by God to resurrect the righteous and unrighteous, fulfilling God promises even to the dead (John 11:25; Acts 24:15). The Witnesses do not consider this resurrection to be a second chance because many have lived and died with little or no knowledge about God. Rather, their resurrection affords them their *first* chance to accept God's rulership based on accurate and compre-hensive knowledge about him. Witnesses anticipate teaching resurrected ones as part of "the greatest educational program in all human history" (*Watchtower* 2022: 20).

---

[29] Witnesses hold the commemoration annually, with unleavened bread and red wine as emblems of Jesus' body and shed blood.

[30] All members of the Governing Body of Jehovah's Witnesses belong to this group of 144,000.

Since Jesus played the central role in opening the way for humans to become reconciled to God, prayers to God would henceforth be offered through Jesus. The provision of the ransom is seen both as the superlative expression of God's love for fallen humanity, and of Jesus' love for his Father and for humankind. The aforementioned progression – from humanity's fall into sin to redemption, and the ultimate fulfillment of the divine purpose – is epitomized in the leading petitions of the Lord's Prayer, or Our Father prayer: that God's name be sanctified, or held sacred; that his Kingdom come; and that his will be done on earth as it is done in heaven (Matthew 6:9–13).

## Principled Love as a Doctrinal Foundation

It may sound trite to say that Jehovah's Witnesses point to love as their doctrinal foundation. Love is an elementary teaching of many ethical systems. Humans individually and collectively express love within the concentric circles of their "universe of obligation" (Fein 1979: 4). Affectionate love of family and friends, ardent love of country, and philanthropic love of humanity call for different degrees and expressions of love, loyalty, and sacrifice. Though certainly not unique to Jehovah's Witnesses, biblical conceptions of love function as their central rationale for tangible acts. Thus, to understand Witnesses' identity and their motives, it is important to explore three levels of love that are embedded in their doctrinal understanding and govern their manner of worship, ethical behavior, and social relations. These concepts illuminate Witnesses' relationship to God, their internal cohesiveness as a community, and their orientation toward those not sharing their faith.

Jesus framed love as a Christian obligation: "You must love Jehovah your *God* with your whole heart and with your whole soul and with your whole mind" and "You must love your *neighbor* as yourself" (italics added) (Leviticus 19:18; Deuteronomy 6:5; Matthew 22:37–40). On the night before his death, Jesus gave his disciples a "new commandment": "Love *one another*; just as I have loved you, you also love one another" (italics added) (John 13:34–35). All three commandments use the Greek word *agape,* defined as love guided by principle. This form of love "can be known only from the actions it prompts" (*Vine's* 1981: 21).

Love for God is shown by personal devotion to him and obedience to his standards of justice and morality "as beloved children" (Ephesians 5:1). Principled love of neighbor includes expressing care for people one does not personally know, those with whom one may disagree, and even one's enemies. Jesus set the pattern by preaching the good news about the Kingdom and doing good works without cost. He illustrated this kind of love in the parable of the

Good Samaritan and in his famous Sermon on the Mount. He also expressed love for his enemies by refusing to retaliate when persecuted. Finally, Jesus' new commandment – "love one another just as I have loved you" – required a higher degree of love among his disciples. "No one has love greater than this," he said, "that someone should surrender his life in behalf of his friends" (John 15:12–13). Jesus set the example of self-sacrificing love by his death, and he made such love a requirement for Christians in their family-like relationships with one another.

Jehovah's Witnesses' teaching materials explicitly emphasize principled love as the basis for moral values and ethical conduct. Certain Witness doctrines combine all three aspects of love, such as the Witness position of political neutrality and their individual conscientious objection to war. Jehovah's Witnesses recognize the relative authority of the State and believe it a Christian duty to comply with civil law while remaining politically neutral. In rare cases, however, secular authorities demand what God forbids. Witnesses believe they are not authorized to choose sides in political conflicts or to take any human life. Love for God, fellow believers, and neighbors moves Witnesses to abstain from war. Bruno Knöller, who refused to serve in the Nazi Wehrmacht, stated: "It was unthinkable for us to take up arms and fight against other people only because the state considered them to be enemies. Even an enemy is worthy to be loved" (Garbe 2008: 350). In conflict settings, Witnesses have met with brutality and death for their refusal to bear arms.

Love for God and respect for the sanctity of life underpin the Witnesses' belief that blood is sacred. The post-Flood prohibition to Noah against shedding human blood also forbade the eating of blood. The law given to the nation of Israel likewise prohibited the eating of blood, and the first-century governing body decreed that Christians abstain from blood (Genesis 9:4–5; Leviticus 17:13–14; Acts 15:28–29). Jehovah's Witnesses apply these verses to the modern medical use of allogeneic (donor) blood. Witnesses' refusal of blood transfusions reflects their belief that the Bible is inspired of God, and therefore, its principles – decreed by the Creator of the human body – are applicable and beneficial even in modern times. Further discussion of this issue is found in the section on interaction with wider society.

Love of neighbor and respect for life are shown not only in mundane matters, such as driving responsibly, maintaining home and workplace safety, and observing public health protocols, but also by avoiding harmful attitudes and acts, such as dishonesty, rage, racial and ethnic hatred, sexual violence, greed, and slander, as well as misuse of tobacco, alcohol, and drugs. Society in general may also frown on the latter practices; but tying the exercise of self-regulation to the obligation to love God and neighbor elevates personal decisions above self-interest alone and dignifies words and deeds as acts of godly devotion.

Although holding what many would consider conservative, outmoded views of morality, Witnesses' belief in individual free will prevents them from forcing their ethical views on others who choose to live differently. Within the family circle, Witnesses believe marriage between man and woman to be permanent and sacred, whether in union with a Witness or non-Witness. Sex is proper only within marriage; sexual infidelity is the only ground for scriptural divorce and remarriage (Matthew 19:3–9; Hebrews 13:4).[31] Sex and procreation exclusively within marriage ideally provides children with committed parents who view child-rearing as part of their moral responsibility. Witnesses moreover hold that God's love extends to the unborn, whose life begins at conception. This view precludes abortion.[32]

For Witnesses, a foremost expression of love of God and neighbor is their public ministry. Observers might assume that Witnesses evangelize to work their way into Paradise, but Witnesses teach that no imperfect human can earn salvation by works. Nevertheless, genuine faith prompts good works. To withhold knowledge of God from others would be selfish (1 Corinthians 9:16). Jehovah's Witnesses believe their religion alone represents true Christianity. However, they do not believe that they are the only ones who will be saved, nor do they expect that simply being a Witness guarantees salvation. At the same time, they believe the Bible sets forth the conditions for salvation, including having faith in Jesus and following his teachings. The well-known passage in John 3:16 presents two possible outcomes: "Everyone exercising faith in [Jesus] might not be destroyed but have everlasting life." The options of eternal life and eternal death are the same choices given to Adam and Eve. How God will judge earth's billions according to his love, mercy, and justice is his decision to make. In obedience to Jesus' command, the Witnesses consider themselves responsible to proclaim the good news of salvation. The rest is between the hearer and God.[33]

Living life in awareness of the issue of universal sovereignty engenders a sense of responsibility toward the Creator and Sovereign, Jehovah God. Dedication to God is a vow not only to live in obedience to his laws but also

---

[31] Legal separation is considered justified when facing physical, sexual, verbal, or emotional abuse, extreme neglect, and similar circumstances (WTBTS-PA 1996: 147, 160–1).

[32] Exceptions include a tubal pregnancy that will not come to term or a medical emergency in which only the life of the child or the mother can be saved in childbirth (*Watchtower* 1975b: 191; WTBTS-PA 1989a: 26). The use of contraceptives is viewed a matter of personal choice (*Watchtower* 2017b: 16).

[33] See "Trust in the Merciful 'Judge of All the Earth'!" and "What Do We Know About Jehovah's Future Judgments?" in the May 2024 issue of *The Watchtower* for recent clarifications about God's judgments.

to promote the interests of his Kingdom. This position has broad implications for the way Witnesses live their lives and how they see their place in the world.

## 3 Identity

Having described Jehovah's Witnesses' beliefs, we now turn to the believers. We discuss the formation of religious identity, processes of decision-making, influence of religion on gender and family roles, and modes of exit from and return to the community.

As sociologist of religion Milda Ališauskienė observed, the identity of religious minorities may be distorted or "othered" when "a dominant group fails to understand that minority identity on its own terms" (Ališauskienė 2023: 166). For example, when public discussion of a minority group is dominated by beliefs and practices that the majority deems controversial, discussion seldom reaches an in-depth analysis of personal, religious, or social identities, or the cognitive and intrapersonal processes involved in identity formation. Anthropologist Anatolii Tokmantcev wrote that much scholarship "flattens our understanding of the actual lived experience of JWs and depicts an unrealistically homogenous group" (Tokmantcev 2023: 20–1). The community of 8.8 million Jehovah's Witnesses extends to nearly every country, making their wide diversity a significant aspect of their individual and collective religious identity. Witnesses make individual life choices in broad areas, including vocation, family life, health, and their degree of involvement in religious activities (Rota 2019). The emic perspective seems a crucial component in analyzing questions of the agency, motivation, and personal autonomy of those belonging to a marginalized, morally conservative religion that entails a relatively high level of commitment.

To explain the basic processes of becoming and identifying as a Witness in social scientific terms, we draw on a framework developed by psychologist Vassilis Saroglou, which describes the "nuanced interplay of how religion works in individuals' lives" (Saroglou 2011: 1321).[34] His four dimensions of "religiousness" are believing (cognition), bonding (emotion/ritual), behaving (morals), and belonging (social network).

Believing: Saroglou proposed that "the basic universal component of religion" is a set of beliefs in the transcendent – that beyond ordinary perception – and its connection to humans and the (tangible) world (Saroglou 2011: 1323). Religious studies scholar George Chryssides noted that while a gap often exists between

---

[34] Among numerous theoretical frameworks for the study of religion, Saroglou's model provides a useful tool for articulating the interconnected psychological dimensions of religion and individual religiosity.

a religion's complex theology and the way its adherents comprehend it, in the case of Jehovah's Witnesses, "there tends to be a closer proximity between official teaching and believers' understanding" (Chryssides 2022: 41). One main reason for this proximity is the process involved in adopting the Witness faith, which involves "an active subject" who is "making meaning" by an extensive study of the religion's beliefs (cf. Streib et al. 2009: 19).

Witnesses offer an interactive Bible study course that aims to provide a basis for belief in the existence of God as humanity's caring Creator. Discussion topics center on God's personality and purpose, basic doctrines, Bible history, the meaning of life, moral values, interpersonal relationships, and congregational worship. Personal Bible studies may continue for months or longer. The majority of those who study with Witnesses do not ultimately become baptized Witnesses. Each individual decides whether to believe or live by Witness precepts. *The Watchtower* states: "No one should feel pressured by a parent, a Bible teacher, or anyone else in the congregation to get baptized. That is not Jehovah's way" (*Watchtower* 2018a: 6–7). Bible teachers and students often form close friendships through their discussions, and some who cease their regular study continue to have occasional spiritual conversations or attend meetings with Witnesses.

According to a 2022 study of Jehovah's Witnesses in Kazakhstan, over 90 percent reported that they could express doubts and questions during their Bible study sessions, and 60.8 percent studied for over a year before baptism, suggesting that "the decision was voluntary and thoughtful" (Auyezbek & Beissembayev 2023: 18). This path to believing bears no resemblance to the sudden conversions or those associated with dubious allegations of brainwashing; rather, it entails learning, reasoning, and deciding (cf. Bromley 2007: 194).

Bonding: Saroglou defines this second dimension as the emotional and ritualistic aspects of religion that connect one to "a deeper reality." Through faith, the believer sees beyond everyday materiality, for instance, by bonding with a deity through prayer (Saroglou 2011: 1326). Psychologists use attachment theory to explore similarities between the process of bonding with a supernatural being and emotional bonding between humans, particularly in parent–child relationships (Paloutzian & Park 2013; Grandqvist 2020; Cherniak et al. 2021). Intimacy, or bonding, with God is a recurring theme in Witness literature and discourse. Witnesses teach that while God loves humanity in general, humans can enter a special relationship with him as their heavenly Father. The bond of dedication and baptism formalizes this connection.

During the course of Bible study, some individuals accept Witness teachings and decide to dedicate themselves to doing God's will. That personal dedication, made in private prayer, is publicly symbolized by water baptism. Before baptism, one first becomes an unbaptized "publisher," a term for one who participates in the public ministry. An active publisher, whether baptized or unbaptized, shares in the evangelizing activity on a monthly basis. Since unbaptized publishers are publicly identified with Jehovah's Witnesses, they are expected to be living according to the moral values of the faith community. Participating in the public ministry before baptism allows individuals to experience what will become a part of their religious identity if they proceed with baptism. Baptism symbolizes one's intimate attachment (bonding) with God, which ideally deepens over time. Before baptism, congregation elders arrange two open-book discussions to review 60 questions and scripture citations summarizing Witness beliefs and practices (WTBTS-PA 2019: 169–212). This review allows the baptismal candidate to demonstrate comprehension of Witness teachings and affirm a personal determination to live by them.

Behaving: Saroglou's third dimension of religiousness involves "specific norms and moral arguments defining right and wrong *from a religious perspective*" (Saroglou 2011: 1326, italics in original). Saroglou observes that historically, religious norms and societal values have often overlapped. However, religion "posits higher moral standards than those of the environing society such as altruistic sacrifice, humility, or strong self-control of impulsivity-related behaviors," with rules regarding "the need for purity and the respect of the divinity" (1327). Moral standards that Witnesses embrace were once common to most religions and cultures but are increasingly viewed by secular, individualistic societies as unduly restrictive (cf. Smith 2003). Though committed to these moral standards, Witnesses are politically neutral and neither lobby for legislative change nor mount pressure campaigns to promote their views.

In scriptural terms, imitation of Christ involves putting on "the new personality" (Ephesians 4:24). For some, this means a significant change in outlook, values, or conduct. For others, including those raised in Witness households, moral norms may be learned and internalized even from a relatively young age (Armet 2009). Witnesses interact regularly with people holding differing moral views. To help Witnesses to maintain their integrity, their publications urge vigilance to avoid attitudes, associates, and actions that may diminish spiritual focus or erode moral resolve. Adolescents are especially susceptible to peer pressure to engage in high-risk behaviors. Conversely, the protective effect of healthy parent–child relationships helps adolescents establish stable friendships and a moral foundation (Bengtson 2013; Lehman & Martinez 2023). Witness parents believe they have a God-given responsibility to provide guidance for their children's social lives. Research into religious socialization and adolescent identity suggests that a parenting style that combines "high moral expectations [and] pro-social and moral development" with "parental responsiveness and warmth" correlates with adolescents' decision to practice the religion in which they were raised (Armet 2009: 291–2).[35]

Many decisions in life are not covered by explicit biblical directives. In so-called gray areas, Witnesses look to Bible principles – "fundamental directives that cover a variety of situations and aspects of life" – to calibrate their conscience and guide their decision-making (*Watchtower* 2002; *Watchtower* 2018c). Personal background and the cultural and situational context may also affect a Witness's conscientious decision. For example, a Witness who has overcome alcohol abuse may decide to avoid alcohol altogether, whereas another Witness may be comfortable with moderate alcohol use.

Belonging: Religion by definition is collectivist, or group oriented (Saroglou 2011). Collective societies usually recognize an authority that defines group norms, goals, duties, and shared beliefs (Stark & Iannaccone 1997). Collective cultures generally prioritize cooperation and unity over personal preferences and goals (Triandis 1995).

The Witness community has been described as "highly integrated, relatively homogeneous in terms of culture, identity and practices." Their customary terms of address – "brother" and "sister" – reflect their ideal concept of belonging to a worldwide spiritual family and the equalizing effect of a social network that improves the "life chances of the socially disadvantaged" who become part of the community (Pachovskyy & Demkiv 2019: 27, 32). Organized activities that characterize Witnesses' religious life, such as large conventions and recorded video events, aim to foster a sense of belonging, which they see as foreshadowing the unity and peace that the human family will enjoy in the new world to come (Tokmantcev 2023). Witnesses' shared identity as citizens of God's Kingdom reinforces their ethical positions of nonviolence and political neutrality.

Recent quantitative studies have found that Witness identity encompasses these four aspects of believing, bonding, behaving, and belonging. Witnesses' most important life values are maintaining a clear conscience and living in harmony with the Witnesses' moral norms, which may correlate to self-reported improved well-being and family relationships after becoming Witnesses. Among the foremost reasons to become and remain Witnesses, respondents chose: to be closer to God, the logic of the teachings, to learn more about the Bible, to make better decisions, and to have a hope for the future. (Auyezbek & Beissembayev 2023; Nkurikiyinka & Chu, forthcoming).[36]

---

[35] See Furstenberg et al. (1999) for a longitudinal case study of Witness parenting in an urban environment.

[36] Responses from Japan, a secularized, non-Christian country, differed somewhat. See Hu and Murata (2024).

## Ministry and Social Roles in Religious Identity

The public ministry is a principal feature of the collective Witness identity and the most visible manifestation of the community's tradition of volunteerism (Pachovskyy & Demkiv 2019).[37] During the 2023 service year (September 2022 to August 2023), Witnesses conducted Bible studies with more than seven million individuals. Witnesses conceive of their evangelizing as life-saving and other-centered altruism, whether people accept their message or not. The faith's doctrinal and moral boundaries could generally be described as distinct and fixed, and yet the doors to the community are open to all people regardless of ethnicity, socio-economic status, or background. Despite the challenge of speaking to strangers about matters of faith, many Witnesses apparently experience fulfillment from their personal ministry. For some, the keen desire to share their faith stems from the transformative effect of biblical teachings on their own lives. Some depictions of high-commitment minority religions portray the witnessing work as largely a product of top-down coercion rather than voluntary motivation (e.g., Holden 2002). Such assumptions presuppose that consistent, large-scale participation could be hardly possible without a high degree of negative social control. However, the plausibility of these assertions is contradicted by millions of Witnesses who participate without pay or other material incentives and at consid-erable cost of their time and resources. The time each publisher spends in the evangelizing activity during each month is a personal matter and is not reported to the organization (except by pioneers).[38] Individual motivations, such as inner satisfaction, personal responsibility, or group belonging, doubtless vary. An analysis of these motives from an emic perspective could illuminate the range of reasons that Witnesses persist in their personal ministry.

Witnesses' degree of investment in their ministry often affects their choices of education and employment, place and type of residence, and use of dispos-able income and leisure time (Cardoza 2021). A number of Witnesses undertake the volunteer ministry as their main vocation rather than professions requiring long periods of university study. Besides their religious activity, most Witnesses have income-earning work to care for their own or family needs (Hu & Murata 2024). The choice of some Witnesses to forgo higher education is not

---

[37] There are no salaried positions in the organizational and congregational structure.

[38] Since 1920, the organization has collected reports on time spent and literature distributed in the ministry to gauge regional progress, generate annual aggregated reports, and plan literature production. However, as of November 2023, publishers simply indicate each month if they shared in the ministry and the number of Bible studies they held. As explained further on, publishers may volunteer for pioneer service, in which case they report hours spent in addition to the number of Bible studies they conducted (*Annual Meeting* October 2023).

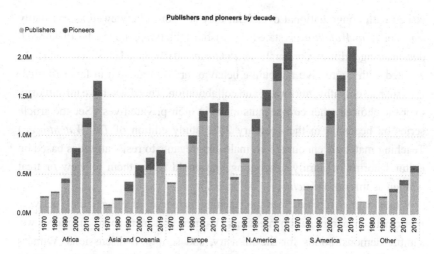

**Figure 1** "Other" includes unnamed lands where Jehovah's Witnesses' religious activity is restricted.

a wholesale rejection of secular education. Witness publications demonstrate respect for both hard and social sciences; academic knowledge is valued but viewed as subordinate to divine wisdom. Consequently, one's identity and self-worth are not bound to educational and employment achievements. About one in six Witnesses worldwide serves as a pioneer, devoting 50 or more hours a month to the public ministry (see Figure 1). A number undertake pioneer service with a view toward additional avenues of volunteer service and training. Witnesses report high levels of subjective well-being and life satisfaction (Namini & Murken 2009; Hu & Murata 2024). The extent to which their public ministry is linked with such ratings is another potential subject for study, especially as correlated with research on volunteerism and altruism (Paxton et al. 2014; Aydinli-Karakulak et al. 2016).

## Gender and Family Roles

Jehovah's Witnesses teach that women and men have equal value and spiritual standing before God. Gender differences are viewed as complementary not competitive in their contribution to family and congregation functioning. At the same time, women do not serve in certain roles involving congregational teaching and governance. Following first-century Christian practice, scripturally qualified men make up a collective body of congregation elders who are responsible for organizing the public ministry, presiding and teaching at congregational meetings, and providing pastoral care. Elders are afforded no reverential treatment, special religious titles, or remuneration; and although tasked with congregational oversight, they are not to be viewed as spiritually superior. *The Watchtower* stated: "Christian elders are not to be dictatorial, domineering, arbitrary, or harsh" (*Watchtower* 2010a: 11). Traits stereotypically equated with aggressive masculine behavior are discouraged in favor of qualities such as empathy, nurturing, and collaboration. The elders have no authority over the choices other congregants make in their private lives. (See the article series on headship in the February 2021 study edition of *The Watchtower.*) Teaching materials encourage all male congregants to resist attitudes based on cultural norms or family upbringing that could cause them to view or treat women as inferior (*Watchtower* 2021: 2–7).

While women do not lead in teaching or serve as elders, they actively participate in congregation meetings. Women and men share in interviews, sample demonstrations for the ministry, and scriptural discussions. Witness women perform the greater proportion of the evangelizing work and comprise the majority of pioneers. Many Witness women worldwide work as volunteer translators, researchers, trainers, and construction workers who participate in building houses of worship (Kingdom Halls). The fact that hundreds of thousands of women elect to engage in these additional activities indicates that they generally find fulfillment, not merely acquiescing to these organizational arrangements (Tokmantcev 2023). The views of Witness women toward their role in the community are another understudied topic.

Gender roles as practiced in Witness families can appear to mirror traditional cultures in which the husband is the undisputed family head. However, Witness literature contains scriptural admonition to Witness husbands to avoid overreaching their authority with controlling, chauvinistic attitudes in family life. A study of Armenian Witnesses observed that women may be attracted to the faith because "JWs' gender rules are equally binding for men and women and therefore are the best version of traditional gender relations" (Tokmantcev 2023: 299). The role of family head entails responsibilities, as articulated in 1 Timothy 5:8: "If anyone does not provide for those who are his own, and especially for those who are members of his household, he has disowned the faith and is worse than a person without faith." This obligation to provide materially for one's family extends to the care of Witness and non-Witness spouses, children, and elderly parents and grandparents (*Watchtower ONLINE*: Study notes) *The Watchtower* emphasizes the gravity of the family head's obligation: "God-fearing men who are able to work do not out of laziness leave it to their wives or older children to provide food and clothing for the family; that responsibility falls squarely upon the shoulders of the family head" (*Watchtower* 1996: 29). On the other hand, applying the "headship" principle does not prevent women from having a secular career.

Extreme physical or material neglect, physical (including sexual) or verbal abuse and violence, mental cruelty, and sexual infidelity are grounds to disqualify one from remaining a Witness. "A man who verbally or physically abuses his wife is anything but manly, and he will lose his relationship with Jehovah" (*Watchtower* 2015a: 22). Witness literature also explicitly condemns culture-bound practices of male domination, such as female genital mutilation; marital rape; child, forced, and polygamous marriage; and dowry-related violence. Materials for congregation study candidly address common behaviors that weaken marriage, such as poor communication, uncontrolled anger, viewing pornography, flirting, and unrealistic expectations.

Witnesses believe God created marriage to be a permanent union. Whether or not one's spouse is a Witness, the scripture applies: "Each one of you must love his wife as he does himself; on the other hand, the wife should have deep respect for her husband" (Ephesians 5:33). Witness husbands are to exercise their responsibilities in a manner that dignifies wives. Witness wives would consider "subjecting themselves" to their husbands as a volitional act of respect (Titus 2:5). About 40 percent of married Witnesses surveyed in Kazakhstan and Japan have non-Witness spouses. Over 99 percent of total respondents, including those in mixed-faith marriages, rate "fidelity" as most important in marriage. In Japan, nearly 80 percent of total respondents consider it unacceptable to divorce over differing religious views, and nearly 90 percent rate their family life as somewhat or very satisfactory (Auyezbek & Beissembayev 2023; Hu & Murata 2024). These findings await cross-cultural comparisons among Witnesses in other countries.

Witness teaching heavily emphasizes the parental responsibility to nurture children emotionally, physically, and spiritually. Rather than holding separate classes or Sunday schools for youths, Witness parents are primarily responsible for their children's religious education, following the biblical pattern of worshipping together as family units (cf. Deuteronomy 31:12). Age-appropriate educational materials for young children as well as for adolescent children reason on biblical principles and cultivate critical thinking skills. Articles and videos discuss how parents can approach sensitive topics with their children, such as sexuality, dating, and body image. Parenting models contrast coercive approaches with effective, open communication that considers each child's emotional, developmental, and situational challenges.

In line with heightened public awareness of the crime of child sexual abuse, the organization has produced videos and publications educating parents and children about protection from sexual predators. In 2019, all congregations studied a series of four *Watchtower* articles that covered the subject, including a discussion of how to support victims of abuse (*Watchtower* 2019a; *Watchtower* 2019b). When requested, Jehovah's Witnesses meet with government officials seeking to strengthen child-protection policies in religious communities. The organization has consulted with child-protection experts to ensure that organizational policies and protocols are compliant with local laws and align with best practices.[39] Congregations maintain no Sunday schools, clubs, orphanages, or other arrangements that separate children from their parents. Congregation elders worldwide are instructed to take steps to protect congregants when handling cases of child sexual abuse. They are to adhere to local civil laws and the organization's policy statement "Jehovah's Witnesses' Scripturally Based Position on Child Protection" (WTBTS-PA 2020; see also National Office for Child Safety 2021).[40]

Witnesses, like most parents, have high aspirations for the happiness and success of their children. Witness literature extols the benefits of prioritizing family and spirituality over material pursuits, achieving a work–life balance (a known predictor of happiness in children), and avoiding the detrimental effects of extreme careerism on family life (Stone & DeRose 2021). Likewise, Witness parents may encourage their children to cultivate such goals as Bible education or humanitarian work (cf. Okun & Kim 2016). Especially in economically disadvantaged areas, Witness parents encourage their children to complete standard education at a minimum and obtain job skills that will allow them to provide for their future family, rather than taking them out of school and subjecting them to child labor to supplement family income.

As children reach maturity, they will make their own decision regarding their religious identity (*Watchtower* 2012: 18–21). Those choosing to live by Witness values may face the challenge of maintaining their identity despite peer pressure (Ringnes et al. 2019; Andersson 2022). The congregation's social network offers an important source of support and the possibility of intergenerational, interethnic, and cross-class friendships that can help youths to develop prosocial attributes and a strong moral core (Pachovskyy & Demkiv 2019; cf. Foulkes et al. 2018; Korkiamäki & O'Dare 2021). Some children raised by Witness parents do not wish to adopt the religion. Such a decision usually does not lead to family estrangement but may cause a measure of disappointment or distress in the family – according to researchers, a fairly common experience among families of various religious traditions (cf. Hendricks et al. 2024). However,

---

[39] See, for instance, Parkinson, Patrick (August 2021). "Expert Report and the Child Protection Policies of Jehovah's Witnesses," https://www.childsafety.gov.au/resources/jehovahs-wit nesses-2021-progress-report and Elliott, Ian. A. (2021). "Child Safeguarding Expert Witness Report on Watch Tower Bible and Tract Society of Britain (Claimant) and the Charity Commission for England and Wales (Defendant). https://webarchive.nationalarc hives.gov.uk/ukgwa/20221215025025/https://www.iicsa.org.uk/key-documents/26619/view/ CJW000126.pdf

[40] The document is published in multiple languages on jw.org.

many youths raised in Witness households sooner or later embrace community values, some to the extent of pursuing lifelong careers in the full-time ministry. Before taking the step of baptism, young and old are encouraged to raise questions and express doubts about what they are learning (Armet 2009). Witness literature describes ways that parents can use the natural inquisitiveness of adolescents as opportunities to build confidence in their abilities to research topics and draw personal conclusions. *The Watchtower* advises: "Discerning parents do not pressure their children to get baptized. Rather, they assist each child to make spiritual advancement in keeping with his or her own growth and progress" (*Watchtower* 2018b: 9).

## Exit and Reentry

Among those who become Jehovah's Witnesses, occasionally some cease their association or religious activity temporarily or permanently. We adapt Saroglou's dimensions to describe possible factors for personal disengagement from the faith or community.

- No longer believing. Disengaged cognitively, doubting the faith's truth claims and God- or Bible-centric belief system
- No longer bonding. Disengaged emotionally, breaking ties with transcendent realities, such as ceasing to pray
- No longer behaving. Disengaged morally, rejecting moral and religious standards of conduct
- No longer belonging. Disengaged socially, discarding collective identity, experiencing conflict or overall dissatisfaction with congregational or organizational arrangements (Saroglou 2011).

Some Witnesses cease their preaching activity or association with the congregation. Witnesses categorize such disengaged ones as inactive and retain hopes that they eventually return to the community. Elders may periodically check on their well-being and offer spiritual assistance. How inactive ones and any Witness friends and relatives handle their relationship is a personal matter. There are no congregation sanctions for inactivity. Some inactive ones maintain ties with Witness friends and relatives. Others sever contact with the congregation and stop living as Witnesses altogether. In a nationwide survey of baptized Witnesses in Rwanda, about 9 percent reported having temporarily discontinued religious activity for unspecified reasons before resuming active participation. Over 50 percent of these returned within two years (Nkurikiyinka & Chu, forthcoming). These findings suggest that many who interrupt the practice of their faith later renew their religious identity as active Witnesses.

A much rarer form of separation from the community is removal from the congregation (formerly called "disfellowshipping"), which may result from serious violation of moral standards, such as sexual misconduct, substance abuse, violence, fraud, and occasionally apostasy, that is, public denigration of the faith or aggressive efforts to turn others against the community. However, removal occurs only if a congregant does not repent of serious sin despite repeated attempts by congregation elders to provide spiritual assistance to help the individual do so. The arrangement is intended to uphold the community's moral standards and protect the congregation from influences that would pose spiritual danger, while moving erring congregants toward repentance and restoration. The ecclesiastical steps for handling cases of serious sin are derived from the process followed by first-century Christians, as described in such passages as 2 Timothy 2:24–25; 1 Corinthians 5:13; and 2 John 9–11 (*Watchtower* 2024c).

The Witnesses' approach is framed in their literature in terms of God's love and mercy, with the objective of helping individuals to fight against sinful tendencies and remain in or return to God's favor. The August 2024 issue of *The Watchtower* contains a full discussion of the scriptural principles and rationale for these ecclesiastical measures, including guidance regarding the exclusionary practice that is occasionally deemed necessary.[41] The recent guidance emphasizes elders' responsibility to assist an erring individual in developing repentance, recognizing that such a process may take time. Elders are instructed to offer assistance with kindness and patience, reflecting God's own attitude toward sinners (*Watchtower* 2024d).

Concerning the ecclesiastical steps, if a baptized adult congregant has engaged in a serious sin, the body of elders selects a committee of at least three elders to determine whether the individual qualifies to remain as one of Jehovah's Witnesses. Removal from the congregation is not a foregone conclusion. Rather, the elders offer to meet with the erring person, perhaps repeatedly, to help him make the required changes. This extended pastoral care allows the person time to reflect, repent, change his behavior, and repair his relationship with God. If wrongdoing has taken place and if it is also considered a crime, the congregation's handling of the matter is not meant to replace actions undertaken by civil authorities.

---

[41] The articles for group congregation study are "Jehovah Wants All to Repent"; "How the Congregation Reflects Jehovah's View of Sinners"; Responding to Sin with Love and Mercy"; and "Help for Those Who Are Removed From the Congregation." (*Watchtower* 2024b: 8–13; *Watchtower* 2024c: 14–19; *Watchtower* 2024d: 20–5; *Watchtower* 2024e: 26–31).

Witness parents have the primary responsibility to give spiritual help and instruction to their children. If a baptized minor under the age of 18 commits a serious sin, it rarely results in removal from the congregation. Two elders would normally arrange a discussion with the minor and his Witness parent(s) or guardian(s) to learn what steps are being taken within the family to help the minor spiritually. If the minor is willing to receive such parental assistance, the elders may decide not to take the matter any further.

If the elders decide that a baptized Witness is to be removed from the congregation, or if he formally renounces his Witness identity by informing the elders that he is disassociating himself and no longer wishes to be known as one of Jehovah's Witnesses, a one-time statement is read to the congregation that the person "is no longer one of Jehovah's Witnesses." No reasons or details are announced. If the removed person is willing to receive pastoral visits, the elders may meet with him a few months later in hopes that he has had a change of heart and has adjusted his moral conduct. If he remains unrepentant, the elders endeavor to reach out to him periodically, offering to pray with him and appealing to him to repent and return to the congregation. In some cases, Witnesses who are removed from the congregation can be reinstated back into the community within a few months. Others have returned after spending many years away (*Watchtower* 2024e).

Removal from the congregation indicates curtailment of socializing within the Witness community, in line with 1 Corinthians 5:11, which says to "stop keeping company" socially with unrepentant wrongdoers. This does not mean total isolation from the community. The individual is welcome to continue attending congregation meetings. Individual Witnesses may decide to invite former Witnesses to meetings and show their goodwill by welcoming the person at the Kingdom Hall. Also, if the person wishes, the elders may arrange for him or her to have Bible study sessions even though he or she has not yet been reinstated into the community. Within the immediate household, kinship ties and filial responsibilities remain, and marriage and family affections continue.[42]

Accepting personal responsibility for one's actions, repudiating serious sin, and resuming meeting attendance are often the first steps toward return. This may be seen as similar to "redemptive processes" in other religions (cf. Pargament & Exline 2022: 256–7), such as acts of penance required in the Roman Catholic Church. Jesus' parable of the prodigal son establishes the Christian attitude toward repentant individuals: The path is always open to reinstatement and spiritual healing (Luke chapter 15).

---

[42] If a married Witness commits sexual infidelity, the Witnesses consider that the innocent mate has the right to decide whether to divorce or remain in the marriage.

While sin, repentance, and ecclesiastical discipline are key themes in Christian theology, the practices of Jehovah's Witnesses have come under criticism, particularly by a vocal minority of disaffected former Witnesses (cf. Wright 2001). A few studies, based on convenience samples recruited primarily via social media, assert a direct causal relationship between the withdrawal of social contact upon disfellowshipping and diminished mental health (e.g., Ransom et al. 2021; Thoma et al. 2023). More systematic research has thus far withheld judgment on causation and has produced mixed results on self-reported levels of improvement or decline in mental health and well-being after disaffiliation from the Witness community (Namini & Murken 2009; Fenelon & Danielsen 2016). Researchers enumerate other factors that may contribute to decline or distress in some following separation from the Witness community, including the loss of the protective benefits of religiosity (e.g., prayer, religious coping, social support), the slackening of previous moral restraints and consequent increase of unhealthy behaviors, and "spiritual struggles" over loss of meaning and purpose in life (Ellison 1991; Fenelon & Danielsen 2016; Pachovskyy & Demkiv 2019; cf. Pargament & Exline 2022). Moreover, when a breach of moral values occurs, as is typically the case with removal from the congregation, the precipitating cause – (mis)conduct without apparent remorse – would also merit consideration of other factors shown to produce negative outcomes, such as guilt and shame, and inner distress over having violated one's own values (called agential moral injury). This kind of distress can be caused, for example, by marital infidelity that leads to a breakdown of the family relationship (Graham 2017).

Feelings of distress may stem from a "bad conscience" that, as Namini and Murken note, is not necessarily damaging but may actually indicate a move toward "taking responsibility and regretting one's misdeeds and may thus spur a person in a positive way" (Namini & Murken 2009: 577). Conversely, "the lack of moral struggle surrounding immoral actions may signal serious problems rather than strength" (Pargament & Exline 2022: 245). Nonreligious psychosocial factors, including family dynamics, parent–child estrangement, and mental states that predate or are unrelated to religious affiliation, also cannot be dismissed as possible contributors to perceived distress upon disaffiliation (Rochford et al. 1989; Namini & Murken 2009; Hendricks et al. 2024).

In social groups large and small, behavioral norms are supported by sanctions imposed for socially harmful actions. Among Jehovah's Witnesses, those who commit an unrepentant breach of community values may consequently experience the loss of a supportive social network within the Witness community, although they will be welcomed at congregation meetings and offered spiritual support by congregation elders. Congregants may also experience pain over the disrupted relationship or feelings of betrayal due to an offender's actions. From the Witnesses' perspective, however, those removed from the congregation are still owed the decency and respect for personal dignity that Witnesses are enjoined to show toward humanity as a whole.

Broadly speaking, departure from the cohesive environment of the Witness community for some may mark a shift from collective values to individualistic ones. A person who is no longer (or never was) committed to the faith could see coercion and control at every turn, resenting spiritual guidance as undue pressure. Moral standards once seen as an incentive toward virtue may now seem to impede personal freedom. Volunteer work could seem like wasted opportunities. Relationships with committed adherents could feel stifling and irritating as compared to other companions whose values and behaviors may be more appealing to one leaving the faith. Much research on disaffiliation from the Witness faith tends to generalize negative effects not only to all who exit the community but even to those who remain. Disenchanted voices depict life in the Witness community as a joyless existence, devoid of personal choice, genuine commitment, and inner satisfaction; and a minority have turned their views into a public campaign against the faith (Chryssides & Gregg 2019; Introvigne & Richardson 2023). Yet, as Bromley stated: "Effects of group membership cannot be judged by examining the state of only those who have left the movements" (Bromley 2007: 44). Indeed, recent studies suggest that Witnesses in general find their religious life satisfying and purposeful. (See concluding section.)

Related to this finding is the fact that a significant proportion of individuals who cease association with Jehovah's Witnesses eventually decide to return (Hu & Murata 2024). The perspective of those who reaffiliate with the Witness community could broaden understanding of the role of moral standards in forming and maintaining religious identity and fulfilling individuals' religious needs.

## Witnesses by the Numbers

According to Witnesses' official statistics, active baptized and unbaptized publishers numbered 8.8 million in 2023.[43] The annual reports reflect what is central to the community identity – sharing their faith. Overall growth has slowed over time but continues despite increasing secularization and the challenges of economic, health, and safety insecurities. Individuals of diverse ages,

---

[43] See jw.org for annual statistics in Service Year Reports and yearbooks of Jehovah's Witnesses. See Stark and Iannaccone (1997) on the reliability of official Witness statistics.

cultures, and socioeconomic backgrounds continue to identify themselves as Jehovah's Witnesses.

Scholars note that in several large surveys, respondents who self-identify as Jehovah's Witnesses outnumber official figures of publishers by wide margins (Stark & Iannaccone 1997; Lawson & Xydias 2020). These individuals could include inactive publishers and former Witnesses, present or former Bible students, never-baptized children of Witnesses, and other sympathizers. Further study is needed about the possible presence of this cohort in survey data.

Table 1 lists notable surveys that include counts of respondents who self-identify as Jehovah's Witnesses (in contrast to most surveys that aggregate Witnesses into categories such as "Other Christian" or "Other Religion"). We note that the number of responses is often too small to generalize to the entire community. For example, the 22 Witness respondents in the US 2021 General Social Survey cannot be divided into smaller groups for meaningful statistical analysis.[44]

Hence, caution is needed in analyzing survey data and conclusions drawn from existing research about minority religions. Research produced with refined methodology and cultural literacy could further understanding of what belonging means to Jehovah's Witnesses and how their religious identity influences the way they see themselves and others.

## 4 Organization

As discussed in the previous section, the religious identity of individual Jehovah's Witnesses involves a learning process with the objective to establish a personal, intimate friendship with God. However, Christianity by its nature entails a communal system of beliefs and values. Using such collective metaphors as body, flock, and familial ties, the Scriptures convey the idea of a community characterized by oneness and cooperation. For the Witnesses, organization provides a framework for the practice of their religion, including the work of global evangelization that is at the heart of their collective identity. This section explores the structure and core functions of Jehovah's Witnesses' organization and discusses its significance in the lives of individual adherents. This overview is not intended to be self-promotional but to describe in broad strokes activities and arrangements that impact the lives of virtually all Witnesses. These global facets of Witness life offer largely untouched territory for further scholarly inquiry in a wide range of fields.

---

[44] It should be noted that not only does the wording of questions about religious identity or membership vary among major surveys, but some survey questions and responses are inconsistently coded individually or in aggregate (e.g., the World Values Survey and International Social Survey Programme).

**Table 1** Notable social surveys that include self-identified Jehovah's Witnesses

| Survey name and organization | Countries | Years | Most recent survey year | Most recent number of self-identified JWs | Most recent total number of respondents |
|---|---|---|---|---|---|
| Afrobarometer. University of Cape Town; Center for Democratic Development (Ghana); Michigan State University (Afrobarometer 2023) | 34 countries 24 coded JWs | 1999–2022 8 waves | 2022 | 317/35085 (0.90%) | 48,084 |
| American Religious Identification Survey. Trinity College, Hartford, Connecticut, USA (Kosmin & Keysar 2009) | USA | 2001, 2008 | 2008 | 312 (0.57%) | 54,461 |
| General Social Survey. National Opinion Research Center at U. Chicago (GSS 2021) | USA | 1972–2021 (bi)annual | 2021 | 22 (0.55%) | 4,032 |

**Table 1** (cont.)

| Survey name and organization | Countries | Years | Most recent survey year | Most recent number of self-identified JWs | Most recent total number of respondents |
|---|---|---|---|---|---|
| General Social Survey: Religion by Gender and Age. Statistics Canada (Cornelissen 2021) | Canada | 1931–2021, by decade | 2018 | 59[1] (0.38%) | 15,660 |
| International Social Survey Programme (ISSP) GESIS Leibniz Institute for the Social Sciences (ISSP 2020) | 33 countries 5 coded JWs | 2017–2020 | 2020 | 44/8233[2] (0.53%) | 46,268 |
| World Values Survey (Haerpfer et al. 2022) | 111 countries or societies | 1981–2022, 7 waves | 2017–2022 | 138[2] (0.15%) | 94,278 |
| YouGov Theos Survey (YouGov 2020) | UK | 2011, 2020 | 2020 | 4 (0.18%) | 2,226 |

[1] Calculated from published survey summary

[2] JWs not coded consistently

The underlying concept of organization is found in the Witness doctrine about God's purpose for the earth – to populate it with a unified human family undivided by borders, nationalities, or warring factions. Jehovah's Witnesses regard all humans as potential members of this global family in which cultures, races, and ethnicities coexist harmoniously. Despite their diverse backgrounds, Witnesses have a strong sense of kinship, even with fellow believers they have never met. The practice of Christianity does not merely entail an individual's acceptance of doctrines or rites. The organization serves as a unifying arrangement – a glue – meant to bind believers together in brotherly love – *philadelphia* – based on their common faith. In line with Witnesses' eschatological expectations, many organizational innovations are intended to further the community's efforts to offer religious education to all peoples. Witnesses point to biblical precedents in which God organized worshippers, as he did with the nation of Israel, to carry out his purpose by a divinely prescribed pattern. More important, Jehovah's Witnesses see their organizational legacy in the practices of the early Christians (cf. 1 Corinthians 14:33, 40). They consider their administrative arrangement a fulfilment of Jesus' prophecy that he, as head of the congregation, would guide and teach his disciples during the time of the end.

## Administering a Global Organization

The Witnesses, like other religious groups, have an organized structure to accomplish community objectives, as well as to handle doctrinal questions, administration of personnel, and expenditure of donated funds. The Governing Body takes the lead in dispensing "food," or spiritual guidance, to the faith community. Based at Jehovah's Witnesses' world headquarters in the town of Warwick, New York, United States, members of the Governing Body represent a range of backgrounds. While they are not chosen expressly to mirror the community's demographic profile, their extensive experience, travel, and interactions help them identify with and respond to the spiritual needs and interests of Witnesses worldwide. Currently serving members of the Governing Body select new members according to the needs of the organization.

Over the decades, the Witnesses have grown into a religion of global proportions (see Figure 2). To accommodate the community's increasingly diverse needs, six committees at world headquarters oversee specific responsibilities: The Coordinators' Committee, Personnel Committee, Publishing Committee, Service Committee, Teaching Committee, and Writing Committee are each composed of several Governing Body members. Assistants advise each committee and implement its decisions (Jehovah's Witnesses – Official Website n. d.-b). Currently, 345 full-time volunteers work directly under these six

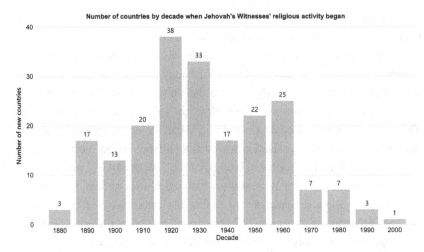

**Figure 2** Approximate years when the religious activity of Jehovah's Witnesses began in countries listed in the 2022 Service Year Report (not including 33 unnamed countries with government restrictions). Numbers are approximate due to changing borders and country names, and limited documentation.

committees. They are of 87 nationalities and speak 156 languages. (These figures and those that follow are current as of 2023.)

Around the globe, 86 branch offices care for Witnesses in 239 countries and territories. Branch offices are overseen by Branch Committees, composed of male elders who typically come from the regions overseen by the branch, as well as from other lands. Committees range in size from three to over twenty. Most committee members have had long association with the faith, as shown by their average years since baptism (43) and average years in full-time volunteer work (35). As is common among Witnesses in general, approximately three-fourths of Branch Committee members were raised from youth (18 and under) in Witness households (see Figure 3).

Branch offices provide ecclesiastical guidance to congregations, supervise the preaching work, and organize large conventions. They coordinate construction projects and disaster relief, and they oversee the translation of publications and videos into local languages. Branches are staffed by 23,680 full-time volunteers (approximately 60 percent male and 40 percent female) in live–work environments, where they receive a small stipend, free room and board, and healthcare assistance. Many more self-supported, part-time volunteers commute or work remotely in support of branch operations. Few positions require academic credentials; but the organization provides professionalized

**Branch Committee members raised in Jehovah's Witness households**

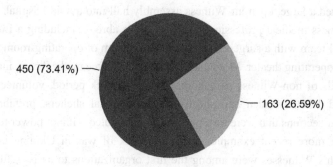

**Figure 3** Of 613 respondents, 450 report having been raised from youth (18 or younger) by relatives who were Jehovah's Witnesses.

training as needed for different roles, whether in technology, administration, construction, finance, or other. By working at branch offices, young Witnesses often develop specialized vocational and social skills that benefit their families and local communities if they later enter the job market.

The organization maintains more than 70,000 facilities for religious activities and builds or renovates an average of five Kingdom Halls per day. The organization's building designs incorporate environmental/sustainability principles, utilizing energy efficient systems and renewable technologies (e.g., Jehovah's Witnesses – Official Website 2017). Local building materials are used where possible (cf. Bocci 2019). Regional or international crews, including skilled tradespersons, work with and train local volunteers. Worldwide, 10,000 full-time construction and maintenance volunteers collaborate with 600,000 part-time workers. While 62 percent of full-time construction workers are male, females comprise over half of part-time construction workers.

Construction volunteers make up a trained global workforce that can be quickly mobilized for humanitarian work in cases of disaster, political or civil unrest, or public health crisis. Jehovah's Witnesses are not a relief organization per se; therefore, few may be aware that they have a standing worldwide arrangement to coordinate relief efforts with a reserve of 100,000 volunteers. Branches proactively contribute to relief efforts through Disaster Relief Committees (DRCs), which are trained to quickly assess needs and implement measures for medical, recovery, reconstruction, and resettlement aid, primarily for Witnesses and their relatives. In so doing, DRCs cooperate with government officials and supplement general relief efforts by humanitarian organizations.

The catastrophic 2010 earthquake in Haiti offers one case study. One day after the quake, the branch office in the Dominican Republic delivered the first of many relief shipments for Haitian Witnesses. Several days later, workers converted a large, open-air Witness assembly hall into a field hospital. Nearly 80 Witness medical professionals arrived from abroad, including a European medical team with a surgeon, an anesthetist, a team of operating-room nurses, and an operating theater. More than 1,000 received free medical care, including hundreds of non-Witness neighbors. In one 10-week period, volunteers constructed 1,500 wooden and sheet-metal transitional shelters, prefabricating modular sections that were transported and assembled without power tools.

As a more recent example, at the outbreak of war in Ukraine in 2022, Jehovah's Witnesses were among the first organizations to assist refugees at the border. DRCs from different countries have conducted joint operations, arranging accommodations for over 55,000 refugees, Witnesses and non-Witnesses. Within Ukraine, DRCs have delivered relief aid, some of it in active combat zones, and have organized evacuations of those unable to flee on their own.

At the outbreak of the COVID-19 pandemic, branch offices facilitated the organizational response by assessing local conditions and helping the Witness headquarters to develop and implement safety protocols worldwide, including the halt of in-person meetings and ministry. About 950 DRCs supported distribution of food, and hygiene and medical supplies. Regular video updates by the Governing Body, broadcast in hundreds of languages on the official website jw.org, urged trust in and compliance with science-based public health directives concerning physical and mental health (Chu 2023). Congregants receive regular reminders regarding disaster preparedness, public health measures, and personal safety.

## Local Congregations in Jehovah's Witnesses' Religious Life

The local congregation forms the social nucleus of the Witness community. The congregation organizes Bible educational work through personal visitation and mobile literature carts in public spaces. Each congregant personally decides the amount of time spent in this voluntary work. Micro-level studies often note the solidarity among Witnesses; participation in the public ministry is an important catalyst in promoting camaraderie and close friendships (e.g., Cardoza 2021).

Congregations worldwide hold two weekly meetings at the Kingdom Hall. The meeting "Our Christian Life and Ministry" consists of Bible study, training for the public ministry, and principles for Christian living. The second meeting, held typically during the weekend, begins with a thirty-minute Bible lecture followed by a one-hour, audience-participation discussion of a *Watchtower* article. No collections are taken at any religious services, nor do the Witnesses practice tithing.

The spiritual needs of each congregation are cared for by a body of elders, the size of which depends on the number of qualified candidates. As with all organizational roles, elders are unpaid. They typically have secular employment and are not required to have formal seminary education.[45] Nevertheless, they need to be well versed in Bible teachings and have adequate experience in religious life. Their personal lives must be lived in line with scriptural qualifications: "moderate in habits, sound in mind, orderly, hospitable, qualified to teach, not a drunkard, not violent, but reasonable, not quarrelsome, not a lover of money, a man presiding over his own household in a fine manner" (1 Timothy 3:1–7; Titus 1:6–9). Following the apostolic model, new elders are appointed by traveling ministers, or circuit overseers, based on recommendations by local bodies of elders. The circuit overseers are assigned by the branch office to visit each congregation twice a year for mutual edification.

Elders offer pastoral support during times of personal crisis and grief, and perform weddings, funerals, and hospital visitations. They are regularly admonished to treat congregants with dignity, respect, and empathy. Elders are not to be "masters over others' faith," nor are they "spiritual policemen" responsible for monitoring congregants' lives (2 Corinthians 1:24). At times, as explained earlier, elders administer ecclesiastical discipline for those who unrepentantly engage in grievous conduct that involves severe physical, moral, emotional, or spiritual harm to others, including victimizing relatives or friends.[46] Especially when providing pastoral care to the vulnerable, such as victims of physical or sexual abuse, the elders are instructed to show special consideration and sensitivity. When offering counsel to a female congregant, an elder may not do so alone. Female congregants may opt to have a close female relative or friend present. Congregants who struggle in their personal lives or who have acted in a way that troubles their conscience may seek support from elders who aim to aid wavering ones to regain their spiritual balance and faith.

## Educational Programs to Meet Organizational Needs

In addition to educational programs at congregation meetings, training programs are provided for those filling certain organizational roles. The Watchtower Bible School of Gilead, established in 1943 for missionary

---

[45] See *Watchtower* 1971: 681–701 for a discussion of the first-century precedent and the present arrangement of congregation elders.

[46] As noted in the identity section, the organization has specific protocols in place for elders in dealing with cases of sexual abuse of children.

training, exemplifies the organization's internationality with the students, male and female, being drawn from all continents and representing a variety of cultures. The early years of Gilead school coincided with the era of decolonization. Instructors emphasized that Gilead-trained missionaries were not to be agents of westernization but were to respect indigenous communities and cultural pluralism. For decades, Gilead graduates were sent to evangelize among diverse populations; but since 2011, graduates have typically been assigned organizational roles, such as administration, translation, and other capacities at the branch or international level. About 60 percent of Branch Committee members are Gilead graduates. Before school commences, students read the entire Bible. The five-month course includes in-depth historical, exegetical, doctrinal, organizational, and practical lessons.

Worldwide, three other ongoing schools have provided instruction for more than 800,000 students in the last decade: the School for Kingdom Evangelizers, a two-month course for (male and female) pioneers; the one-month School for Circuit Overseers and Their Wives; and the one-week School for Congregation Elders. Millions of pioneers have attended Pioneer Service School, a one-week course they can take every five years. Curriculum for all schools emphasizes the application of scriptural principles in organizational and educational activities, and the continued cultivation of Christian values.

## The Channel for Definition and Dissemination of Beliefs

With the emphasis on unity within the faith community, it follows that Witnesses' doctrines and practices would also be communicated through a single channel. The organization disseminates its official teachings in *The Watchtower* and other publications. The Governing Body oversees the publication of such material through the Writing and Teaching Committees. Writers and researchers ensure that new publications align with current teachings and use consistent terminology. A longtime editorial policy stipulates that writers, editors, and artists, as well as translators, remain anonymous in order to focus on the biblical source of the material rather than on individuals (*Watchtower* 1959: 607).

Witness literature urges readers to nurture their spirituality while navigating the challenges of modern life, with an emphasis on the practicality of Bible principles: how to make wise decisions, find true happiness, cultivate good qualities, and maintain family harmony. Articles and videos provide a window into the struggles and issues that Witnesses face, in common with the general population. For instance, while published comments about the COVID-19 pandemic made clear that mask-wearing and vaccination were matters of personal choice, Witnesses were strongly encouraged to avoid politicized debates and to comply with public health measures based on three biblical principles: (1) respect for governmental authority; (2) placing a high value on life; and (3) avoidance of casual attitudes and premature resumption of activity. Witness publications approach matters regarding social injustice, conspiracy theories, the misuse of technology and social media, environmental degradation, and similar contemporary issues from a biblical perspective.

Printed literature for the public has been a hallmark of the organization since the first Bible Students. The organization has also long utilized multimedia materials beginning with the 1914 film, slide, and audio presentation *Photo-Drama of Creation*, and followed by phonograph recordings, radio, and film produced in multiple languages for worldwide distribution. In 1997, the Witnesses launched their official website, watchtower.org. Now named jw.org, it is presently the most widely translated website in the world, with content in over 1,090 languages. The jw.org website has had an equalizing effect on the worldwide community and their ministry, exponentially increasing the reach of and accessibility to free digital content and serving as a major hub in the religious life of Jehovah's Witnesses. Monthly, hour-long programs include scriptural talks, as well as interviews and regional reports. News items on jw.org report organizational milestones, noteworthy events, disasters, relief efforts, legal cases, and profiles of Witnesses on trial and incarcerated for their faith. Companion study tools, such as the apps *JW Library*, and *JW Library Sign Language*, and *Watchtower ONLINE LIBRARY* facilitate Bible study and provide material for communal worship.

## Unity and Cultural Pluralism

The Witness community follows a unified teaching program whereby all congregations feature the same study material at their meetings. A visitor to a Kingdom Hall in Paris, Buenos Aires, Cape Town, or elsewhere could know in advance precisely what material will be discussed. (A global directory on jw.org lists the locations, languages, and meeting times of congregations worldwide.) Like their denominational counterparts, the same doctrines, values, and principles are taught to believers worldwide. To Witnesses, a coherent message is a factor in achieving the Christian ideal, "one Lord, one faith" (Ephesians 4:5). Such unity, however, does not preclude individuality. The Witnesses' borderless, nonpolitical worldview regards cultural difference not as a boundary but a bridge, as is evident in organizational arrangements such as international conventions that introduce visiting delegates to the cultural and historical richness of host countries.

The Witnesses' culturally pluralistic outlook is found in their publications and programs. Their relevance and international character are made possible by input from branch offices worldwide and a diverse editorial and production staff. Text, illustrations, interviews, videos, and music reflect the community's broad demographic composition. For example, a video production shown at 2023 regional conventions depicted the modern-day situation of African Witnesses, many of whom are or have been refugees due to political violence. Such content serves to increase awareness, empathy, and solidarity among Witnesses across national and cultural boundaries.

Cultural pluralism also involves showing linguistic respect, especially with regard to minority languages. Some 80 percent of Jehovah's Witnesses read the publications in languages other than English. In addition, consumers of Witness literature include the visually and hearing impaired, as well as marginalized and indigenous populations. Witnesses publish material in 105 sign languages; Braille publications in 55 languages; audio descriptions of video programs in over 90 languages; and publications in 157 Amerindian and 24 Romany languages. The Witnesses are the largest producer of publications in certain languages spoken by linguistic minorities. In dozens of these languages, *The Watchtower* is the only periodical published. Currently available in 449 languages, *The Watchtower* is one of the most widely circulated magazines in the world. The work is done by 3,300 full-time translators, many of them in Remote Translation Offices where they can be immersed in the target language and in cultural and linguistic patterns of thought. They are trained to use a culture-based approach to achieve accurate, natural, accessible text.[47]

As the organization expanded translation efforts in the 1970s and 1980s, it proved difficult to purchase software, for instance, to publish in non-alphabetic and right-to-left scripts. Witness volunteers developed composition software now called the Multilanguage Electronic Publishing System (MEPS), which facilitates translation and simultaneous publication in hundreds of languages (*Awake!* 1984; *Awake!* 1986).

Bible translation has been at the forefront of the Witnesses' translation initiatives. The Bible Students had long investigated the work of various Bible translators and newly accessible manuscripts, such as Tischendorf's publication of the *Codex Sinaiticus*. In the late 1940s, the Witnesses began work on a new translation primarily because while the most ancient manuscripts of the Hebrew Scriptures contained the Tetragrammaton (the four Hebrew

---

[47] Witness translation efforts in some minority languages have been the subject of linguistic research. See, for example, Barchas-Lichtenstein (2014), Ouily et al. (2024), and the ENDE CORPUS (2021).

letters for God's name) nearly 7,000 times, Bible translations commonly used "Lord" instead.[48] The modern-language *New World Translation of the Holy Scriptures* (*NWT*), released incrementally between 1950 and 1960, uses the divine name (rendered "Jehovah" in English) in the Hebrew Scriptures. The *NWT* also uses God's name in the Christian Greek Scriptures (New Testament). While relatively rare among Bible translations, a significant number of translators in multiple languages have taken a similar approach. (See Appendices A and C of the online *New World Translation of the Holy Scriptures* [Study Edition] (*NWT* Online n.d.); see also *Watchtower* 2015b: 9–17.) Some *NWT* renderings are based on manuscript research that revealed translation errors and spurious verses in the *King James Version* and other translations, as well as inconsistencies in translating Hebrew or Greek expressions (e.g., *sheol* and *hades*). Like other modern Bible translations, the Witnesses' 2013 revised English edition of the *New World Translation* reflects changes in the spoken language, as well as increased understanding of the original languages based on recent advances in the study of authoritative ancient manuscripts. In February 2020, Witnesses released the *New World Translation* in American Sign Language, the world's first complete sign-language Bible, which is free and downloadable from jw.org.

Capabilities of the electronic age have enabled the Witnesses to distribute free digital content to disadvantaged and remote populations. Among recent innovations is JW Box, a Wi-Fi router and storage system, for use in areas with limited Internet access. First used in Africa, about 24,000 JW Boxes are now used in 46 branch territories, providing 1.4 million Witnesses with wireless downloads of publications and videos in 337 languages. The JW Satellite channel broadcasts programming to Kingdom Halls and homes in sub-Saharan Africa 24 hours a day, 7 days a week, in 32 languages. The main method for distribution of Witness publications, however, is the cumulative effort of millions of Witnesses who voluntarily expend time and resources to spread the Word. Thousands of Witnesses have learned new languages or moved to areas where their language skills are needed.

Considering that many of the foregoing activities are carried out in full public view, it is somewhat surprising that they have attracted relatively little scholarly attention. On the contrary, Jehovah's Witnesses are sometimes described in academic literature as an insular or closed community. The final section of this Element discusses the Witnesses' relationship with wider society.

---

[48] This practice may have followed the Jewish tradition not pronouncing the Tetragrammaton, instead substituting "Lord" (Heb. Adonai). However, Hebrew Bibles commonly contain the Tetragrammaton.

## 5 Interaction

Characterizing Jehovah's Witnesses' interactions in civil societies can be complex. Witnesses are known to be uncompromising about a certain few religious positions. They stand out for not celebrating birthdays or popular holidays, nor do they take part in political activism. Occasionally, they find their faith embroiled in public controversies over healthcare and child-rearing, or the subject of sensational journalism. On the other hand, from an emic perspective, most Jehovah's Witnesses would likely see themselves as ordinary people. Many would say that the prevailing view about them often differs widely from their self-understanding. The disconnect between the two sometimes lies not in describing what Witnesses do or believe, but in appraising the motivations and objectives behind certain acts and ideas. In this section, we explore how Jehovah's Witnesses see their place in the world and in their interactions with the societies in which they live.

## The Concept of "the World"

The biblical concept of the world underpins the Witnesses' doctrinal understanding that governs their place in society. The world, as found in Scripture, usually refers to people, or humankind in general. A famous example of this usage is at John 3:16, where it says that "God loved *the world* so much that he gave his only-begotten Son" (italics added). God has shown good will toward the world by sending Jesus to give his life for people no matter their ethnicity, social status, nationality, gender, or orientation. Jehovah's Witnesses believe that similar expressions of love are basic to the practice of authentic Christianity, for instance, by showing empathy, compassion, and altruism, especially in sharing Christ's message with this "world."

However, other Bible verses contain a completely different usage of the word: "Friendship with the world is enmity with God" (James 4:4); "Do not love either the world or the things in the world" (1 John 2:15); and "The whole world is lying in the power of the wicked one" (1 John 5:19). Moreover, Jesus repeatedly said that his disciples would be "no part of the world" (John 15:19; 17:14–16; 18:36). The world in this context has a negative connotation – humans alienated from God and his ways, will, and standards. Therefore, Jehovah's Witnesses' relationship with the world is nuanced: One should love people in the world but maintain distance from the world and its negative influences (WTBTS-PA 2018c).

Some scholars have applied Roy Wallis' typology of a world-rejecting religion to Jehovah's Witnesses. It is of note that Wallis' classic 1984 work posits no definition of world, in either an etymological or a religious sense. Owing to the well-defined boundaries of their community, Witnesses are sometimes described as aloof, or even more critically, as a closed society or total institution (e.g., Holden 2002). Other scholars dispute this characterization. Chryssides (2016) argued against applying the world-rejecting label to Witnesses because they are part of general society and do not live in isolation. Witnesses do not reject secular institutions but obey civil law. Witnesses are not called upon to surrender all their possessions and live as ascetics. Barker wrote: "There are many communities and institutions that are as, or more, 'closed' than the JWs. Unlike many 'closed communities,' JWs do not live together. . . . The vast majority have 'ordinary' secular jobs and live in 'ordinary' nuclear families" (Barker 2023: 4). Psychologist Raffaella Di Marzio concluded: "Though not being 'of' the world ... Jehovah's Witnesses live and work 'in' the world (John 17:14), to which they incessantly present and propose a way of community life, with solid religious values and a substantial set of doctrines" (Di Marzio 2020: 86; Simard-Émond 2023).

One way to understand Jehovah's Witnesses' relationship with society and local communities is to examine their actions and behavior in different contexts.

## In the Public Eye: Interactions in In-Group/Out-Group Relationships

Barker observed: "Jehovah's Witnesses [are] one of the more controversial religions of modern times, but just as controversial are the social reactions to which they have given rise in the numerous countries throughout the globe in which they are found" (Barker 2023: 4). This is to say, controversies about Jehovah's Witnesses are sometimes based mainly on differences of opinion and values. At times, challenges to Witness positions stem from societal prejudices, incomplete information, or rejection of religiously motivated values. Careful scholarship can bring greater clarity by elucidating perplexing practices, deconstructing stereotypes, demythologizing idealistic portrayals, but most importantly, in our view, by illuminating the lives and views of ordinary Witnesses. Although it may be assumed that conservative religious traditions impose a preponderance of rules, Witnesses are far more often guided by a moral framework of general principles in many areas of life. Their personal choices vary widely in social relations, work careers, recreation, education, or dress and grooming. Witnesses regard dress and grooming as part of their message meant to reflect dignity, respect, and consideration of local customs.

Beyond the impact of their personal decisions on themselves, Witnesses are encouraged to contemplate their decisions' effect on their relationship with

God, and the impact on the consciences of others. For example, refusing to watch degrading entertainment or engage in dishonest business practices would be motivated by their awareness of what pleases and displeases their Creator and Life-Giver, and the wish to avoid negative effects on their attitude and behavior toward their neighbor. Witnesses are keenly aware that their actions may undergo greater scrutiny because of their public ministry and minority status. This can be both positive and negative. Survey respondents in Japan rated "Jehovah's Witnesses' good-hearted qualities" as the foremost reason for having accepted the faith (Hu & Murata 2024).

One way in which Jehovah's Witnesses seek to contribute to the stability of society as a whole is by fulfilling their family responsibilities. In his socio-historical study on Witnesses, Artur Artemyev (2021) suggests that the intellectual environment Jehovah's Witness families provide to their children promotes their general interest in knowledge and studying. Bible-based parenting materials explain how to teach children prosocial attributes and skills, such as communication, decision-making, emotional coping and self-regulation, generosity, and resilience. Avoidance of marital infidelity, alcohol abuse, gambling, uncontrolled anger, materialistic excess, and similar harmful or wasteful practices enables Witness families to direct financial and emotional resources to the nurturing of healthy family relationships. Witnesses, like most people, raise their children according to their own values and worldview. While some values, such as honesty, may be considered universally acceptable, certain biblical values embraced by Witnesses are not shared by the majority of society. Although the parental right to teach religious values to children is affirmed by international standards, these rights are increasingly being challenged. A Witness who is married to a non-Witness is expected to respect his or her spouse's convictions and views regarding child-rearing. Non-Witness spouses often do not object to Bible-based moral and spiritual education for their children. Some Witnesses, though, face strong opposition from non-Witness family members. Even so, Witnesses are taught ways to show consideration and respect with the aim of reducing tensions and improving mutual understanding.

While Jehovah's Witnesses apply to themselves a set of values and moral standards, they are enjoined to respect others' right to live as they choose. For example, although one research survey indicated that three-fourths of Witnesses think that homosexuality should be discouraged, they do not sponsor legislation to force others to live according to their values (Pew Research Center n.d.). They might disagree with others about ideological opinion, moral outlook, or sexual orientation; but the Golden Rule has no exceptions. Witnesses believe that no one should be denied the opportunity to hear their Bible message, which they consider as beneficial and potentially life-saving. They conduct Bible courses with hundreds of thousands of people whose life choices do not harmonize with theirs. "In their case, 'separateness' and 'difference' do not mean opposition or hostility, but rather consistency of faith and an offer of salvation" (Di Marzio 2020: 86).

## Bloodless Medicine

To Jehovah's Witnesses, life is a sacred gift to be preserved by all reasonable means. They do not practice faith healing, nor do they believe in miraculous cures in modern times. While they accept the vast majority of medical procedures and therapies, Witnesses have become well known to clinicians for their refusal of allogeneic (donor) blood transfusions, based on their understanding of Bible passages that prohibit taking in blood to sustain the body. However, a range of medical practices may be acceptable to many Witnesses, such as the use of a patient's own blood during a medical procedure, provided there is no advance storage. Regarding the medical use of derivatives (minor blood fractions) of any of the primary components of blood, Witnesses make personal decisions according to their religious conscience.

As an alternative to blood transfusions, Witnesses have turned to what is called bloodless medicine and have developed a structured and consistent approach in order to facilitate communication with the medical community. For Witness patients and the clinicians who treat them, the Witness organization has a free information-sharing network of about 2,000 Hospital Liaison Committees (HLCs) in 110 countries, as well as an extensive online library with peer-reviewed articles and evidence-based clinical strategies (Jehovah's Witnesses – Official Website n.d.-a). Working with Hospital Information Services at world headquarters, local HLCs interact with medical professionals and Witnesses desiring treatment that respects their religious views. Assistance by HLCs is available to Witness patients upon request. The HLCs have been described as "straightforward, nonconfrontational, and helpful" as they "assist doctors in reaching an individualized agreed strategy" by providing information on preoperative and perioperative blood conservation measures (Hivey et al. 2009: 944). Some medical professionals see the HLC arrangement as potentially coercive, whereas others evaluate the arrangement as beneficial to medical practice and patient outcomes.[49] Witnesses themselves underline that the HLC arrangement is designed to support individual Witnesses who request assistance in communicating with medical professionals to ensure that they receive quality care and respect for their rights and wishes.

---

[49] See "Blood," chapter 5, in Knox (2018: 148–201).

Jehovah's Witnesses' stand on the medical use of blood is motivated by religion, not by science. Nevertheless, many landmark scientific studies published in the last two decades have found that the use of evidence-based medical treatment strategies that minimize blood loss, manage anemia, and avoid blood transfusion has been associated with increased safety and superior clinical outcomes, including reduced morbidity, shorter hospital stays, lower mortality, and decreased costs (Leahy et al. 2017; Althoff et al. 2019). Some clinicians have decades of experience in treating patients successfully without the use of blood-based therapies, including programs for bloodless medicine and surgery (also called "patient blood management").[50] Medical professionals with experience in the systematic and optimal use of blood conservation and transfusion-alternative strategies state that the lessons learned "are likely to benefit all patients, given recent evidence suggesting that patients who avoid ABTs [allogeneic blood transfusions] do as well, if not better, than those who accept transfusions" (Resar & Frank 2014: 553; cf. WHO 2021). The Witnesses' position on avoidance of blood therapies has influenced the field of bioethics in the areas of patient autonomy and the right to treatment (Mattei 2023).

## Political Neutrality

The famous dialogue between Jesus and Roman governor Pontius Pilate encapsulates Jehovah's Witnesses' view of political involvement. During his trial, Jesus told Pilate: "If my Kingdom were part of this world, my attendants would have fought" (John 18:36). In this context, Jesus spoke of having no part in the political structures of the world. For Jehovah's Witnesses, Jesus' statement signifies the Christian requirement to remain neutral, neither taking up arms nor participating in political conflicts, whether ideological or ethnic in nature. Giving allegiance to any political party or ideology would directly conflict with their strong conviction that God's Kingdom is an existing, heavenly government that will accomplish its purposes in governing the earth. And taking up arms to kill in the name of a nation-state, ethnic or political entity, or ideology would contravene both the precedent Jesus set and God's commandment to love one's neighbor as oneself. Supporting rebellion or violence against civil authority would also violate the Witnesses' concept of neutrality.

In their exercise of political neutrality, Jehovah's Witnesses seek to balance their responsibilities to God and the State. While they refuse military service, Witnesses seek open communication with officials to make clear that their stance is not intended as civil disobedience. Where available, Witnesses

---

[50] See Farmer et al. (2023) for an accessible overview of patient blood management by leading practitioners and proponents.

participate in alternative civilian service programs that do not violate their conscientious position (*Information on Conscientious Objection* n.d.).

In times of war or under totalitarian regimes, Jehovah's Witnesses' political neutrality has provoked severe government reaction. Their doctrine on military service (then as Bible Students) was shaped by World War I. Soon after the Military Service Act of 1916 introduced compulsory service in the United Kingdom, 264 Bible Students applied for exemption as conscientious objectors. Some were court-martialed and sentenced to up to ten years of penal servitude (Perkins 2016). Soon after World War II began, the Witnesses further articulated their nonnegotiable neutrality toward politics and military service (*Watchtower* 1939). Witnesses, male and female, underwent brutal treatment in Axis countries during the 1930s and 1940s (WTBTS-PA n.d.; Hesse 2001; Wah 2002). The persecution peaked in Nazi-occupied Europe, where about 13,000 suffered incarceration in prisons and concentration camps and 600 children were removed from parental custody. About 1,750 Witnesses died, 548 of them by execution – mostly for conscientious objection. Postwar Communist regimes systematically oppressed Witnesses, with thousands imprisoned and deported to Siberian forced-labor camps (Dirksen 1999; Baran 2014). The fact that the organizational center of the Witnesses is in the United States has fueled anti-Witness persecution in countries that suspect local Witnesses of working for US intelligence services. Several African dictatorships launched brutal persecution during the 1970s and 1980s. Eritrean Witnesses still endure torture and lengthy imprisonments without charge. In 2017, some 175,000 Witnesses in Russia came under a nationwide ban for "extremism," a bitter irony for a faith that has held to its uncompromising ethic of nonviolence for more than a century. The US Commission for International Religious Freedom reported that "state persecution of Jehovah's Witnesses has increased dramatically in recent years," their conscientious objection being the core issue (USCIRF 2020: 1).

Nevertheless, Witnesses see themselves as peaceful citizens who pose no threat to the social or political order. Relatively speaking, few governments have categorically demanded that Witnesses violate their neutrality by serving in the military or voting in elections. One can argue that there is an inevitable clash of ideologies: From the nation-states' point of view, by not adhering to all government mandates, the Witnesses are challenging the political order. However, even in polarized and politicized environments, they believe they should adhere to their nonviolent ethic. Witnesses as a group refuse to harm others even under threat of death, such as occurred during the Genocide against the Tutsi in Rwanda in 1994 (Chu & Seminega 2022).

## Preaching and Teaching

Jehovah's Witnesses are most known for their religious educational work, carried on door-to-door and in public places. While their primary objective is spiritual in nature, Witnesses see their work as providing practical benefits to the social, health, and familial situations of people in their community. Through their ministry, Jehovah's Witnesses proactively reach out to hundreds of people in their localities. The results of these interactions should not be measured in terms of the number of conversions. For example, in 2023, Witnesses conducted 7.3 million personal Bible study courses worldwide, while the number of those baptized that year was about 270,000. Some 20.5 million attended Jehovah's Witnesses' annual commemoration of Jesus' death, more than double the number of active Witnesses. Evidently, millions of individuals who do not become baptized Witnesses wish to benefit from free Bible instruction in various ways.

In pursuing their main objective of Bible education, Jehovah's Witnesses' conduct free literacy programs to enable people to read the Bible for themselves. Beginning in the late 1940s, congregations have held literacy classes in many African lands, with thousands of women being the main beneficiaries. Since 1946, in Mexico, the Witnesses have taught more than 152,000 people to read and write in Spanish. Witnesses have distributed 224 million brochures in 720 languages for those with limited education. In many countries, Jehovah's Witnesses conduct prison ministries to help prison inmates reform and improve their life prospects. In 2022, Witnesses in Brazil held Bible studies with 208,000 inmates. A recent study concluded that their "voluntary charity work" has "become an additional mechanism for their integration both into the public sphere of society and in cooperation with state bodies" (Pachovskyy & Demkiv 2019: 32). In short, Witness volunteerism is central to the community's interactions with wider society.

However, organized opposition to the Witnesses' preaching work has occasionally arisen, often built in a climate of stereotyping and misinformation. This pattern has occurred sporadically over the last 140 years, especially in countries with a dominant or State religion that leverages its political influence. For example, the Orthodox Church in Russia has spearheaded opposition to the Witnesses in the twenty-first century. Adhering to their apolitical position means that Witnesses do not resort to lobbying governments; however, in using the judicial system to ensure their rights and freedoms as guaranteed by law, the Witnesses have proven highly successful.

The reasons for opposition can be analyzed in several contexts. In countries with one hegemonic religion, Witnesses' preaching activity can be viewed as an ideological threat to the traditional religion and its supremacy. Of course, in some cultures or local communities, the opposition toward preaching initiatives stems from nonreligious sources. Harmful rumors or misinformation can create prejudice against Jehovah's Witnesses. Witnesses also understand that some people do not welcome uninvited callers to their homes to talk about religion; some reject their message out of strong religious conviction, skepticism about the Bible, or disillusionment with organized religion. Religion for many is a private matter; hence, Witnesses try to respect people's preferences and search only for individuals who wish to discuss spiritual topics.

## Legal Battles for Freedom of Religion

The Witnesses' abstinence from politics means that they have not sought political influence to protect their rights. However, as the apostle Paul invoked his Roman citizenship in "defending and legally establishing the good news," Jehovah's Witnesses have similarly utilized legal channels to secure rights to which they are entitled as citizens (Philippians 1:7). Why have court cases figured so prominently in the history of Jehovah's Witnesses? Awareness of religious freedoms began evolving during the early twentieth century, creating the need for a legal framework to define them. During this period, Jehovah's Witnesses grew rapidly, expanding to many countries where they worked to obtain legal recognition by providing evidence that: (1) they pose no threat to the social order or government and (2) they are entitled to freedom of religion and other fundamental human rights.

Especially since the 1930s, courts in numerous jurisdictions have ruled on cases involving Jehovah's Witnesses. To date, 311 decisions by national supreme courts and constitutional courts, and 127 international decisions by the European Court of Human Rights (ECtHR), the UN Human Rights Committee (CCPR), and the UN Working Group on Arbitrary Detention (WGAD), have directly or indirectly established Jehovah's Witnesses' right to practice their religion. Typically, these high court victories have been preceded by negative decisions in the lower courts. Scholars acknowledge the Witnesses' unparalleled role in the development of religious freedoms and human rights worldwide (McAninch 1987; Kaplan 1989; Greenhaw & Koby 2005; Knox & Baran, in press). For instance, James Richardson described Jehovah's Witnesses as "a formidable legal force," having "significantly influenced the meaning of religious freedom, especially in the United States, Canada, and in the 47 nations that make up the Council of Europe" (Richardson 2015: 286).[51]

---

[51] Most ECtHR cases involving Jehovah's Witnesses center on violations of Articles 9, 10, and 11 of the European Convention of Human Rights, including cases dealing with state registration,

In the early 1940s, a series of US Supreme Court decisions ruled that Jehovah's Witnesses' evangelizing constitutes no "menace to public peace and order," being equivalent to "worship in the churches and preaching from the pulpits" (*Cantwell v. Connecticut*, 310 U.S. 296 [1940]; *Murdoch v. Pennsylvania*, 319 U.S. 105 [1943]).[52] In *Kokkinakis v. Greece*, the ECtHR in 1993 described the preaching work of Jehovah's Witnesses as respectable, "proper proselytism" and held that freedom to manifest one's religion includes the right to try to convince one's neighbor, an aspect of a democratic society. Otherwise, freedom to change one's religion or belief would likely "remain a dead letter."[53] The historic decision was the culmination of a half-century legal battle fought by Minos Kokkinakis, who was first arrested by Greek authorities in 1938 for violating a law criminalizing "proselytism." Kokkinakis underwent arrest more than sixty times and spent over six years in prisons and on penal islands. The 1993 decision was the first time the ECtHR convicted a country of violating religious freedom, and the case has proven crucial in defining the boundaries of individual religious freedoms under the European Convention on Human Rights.

High courts and international bodies have upheld Jehovah's Witnesses' right to political neutrality. In 2011, in *Bayatyan v. Armenia* (Application no. 23459/03, ECtHR) the Grand Chamber of the ECtHR recognized that conscientious objection is protected under the right of freedom of thought, conscience, and religion. South Korea's Constitutional Court stated in 2018 that "the act of conscientious objection is not an aggression toward the legal order of the social community." It continued: "If a person has formed a genuine inner conviction that opposes warfare and the deprivation of another's life, based on their religious values, world views and morals . . . compelling them to perform military service brings a serious crisis as to their ethical identity" (Constitutional Court of Korea, No. 2011 Hun-Ba379, June 28, 2018). The CCPR has likewise held on numerous occasions that any individual has a right to an exemption from compulsory military service if such service cannot be reconciled with that individual's religion or beliefs and the right to manifest them.

---

taxation, censorship of religious materials, child custody, deportation, confidentiality of medical records, lack of neutrality of the State, conscientious objection, and police interference with public ministry or religious meetings.

52  The latest US Supreme Court victory in 2002 (*Watchtower Bible and Tract Society of N.Y., Inc. v. Village of Stratton*, 536 U.S. 150 [2002]) ruled that an ordinance requiring a permit to engage in door-to-door activity is unconstitutional. https://supreme.justia.com/cases/federal/us/536/150/.

53  *Kokkinakis v. Greece* ECtHR App no. 14037/88 (judgment of May 25, 1993) par. 31. https://hudoc.echr.coe.int/#{%22itemid%22:[%22001-57827%22]}.

In 1943, the US Supreme Court's decision on the flag salute (*West Virginia State Board of Education v. Barnette*, 319 U.S. 624) had a major influence in several countries, including Canada, in creating legislation that respects conscientiously (including religiously) motivated behavior of individual citizens – in this instance, the right not to salute the flag. In some countries, the courts have identified forms of institutionalized prejudice. In 2011, for example, the ECtHR unanimously ruled against the French government regarding a tax specifically levied on Jehovah's Witnesses in the 1990s. Scholars have seen this as an example of a state's discriminatory measures in enforcing secularism upon citizens (Richardson 2015).

Among the most comprehensive court decisions upholding Jehovah's Witnesses' rights are the ECtHR rulings against Russia (2010, 2022).[54] The Russian government banned Jehovah's Witnesses in 2017 as an extremist organization. This current persecution has seen the concurrent use of systematic defamatory propaganda. Currently, 137 Witnesses are imprisoned on pretexts that were clearly refuted by ECtHR rulings. The Court failed to identify any incitement to violence or any insulting, slanderous, or discriminatory statements against members of other faiths in the Witnesses' teachings or publications. Their evangelizing work, the Court said, is entirely legitimate. The Court criticized the vague and unscientific definitions of the concept of mind control and found no evidence of individuals whose right to freedom of conscience had been violated by manipulative methods or psychological violence, as claimed by activist opponents. Rather, to become and live as one of Jehovah's Witnesses is a voluntary and conscious choice based on a person's free will. The ECtHR also confirmed that the Witnesses' medical choices and their abstaining from blood transfusions are legitimate and should be respected.

In summary, Jehovah's Witnesses play an active role in society with their charity work and educational activity. Many high courts have recognized them as a peaceful and law-abiding faith community. Yet, Jehovah's Witnesses have been and continue to be subjected to a recurring pattern of accusations, both in more secularized countries and those with religious majorities. They use legal remedies to defend their rights but also to maintain a constructive dialogue with civil authorities that positively impacts their own freedoms and those of others.

---

[54] *Jehovah's Witnesses of Moscow and Others v. Russia.* No. 302/02, 10 June 2010 (Final: 22 November 2010). European Court of Human Rights, https://hudoc.echr.coe.int/fre#{% 22itemid%22:[%22001-99221%22]}; *Taganrog LRO and Others v. Russia*, Nos. 32401/10 and 19 others, 7 June 2022 (Final: 9 July 2022). European Court of Human Rights, https://hudoc .echr.coe.int/eng#{%22itemid%22:[%22001-142225%22]}. See also *Pindo Mulla v. Spain*, European Court of Human Rights Grand Chamber App no. 15541/20 (judgment of 17 September 2024). https://hudoc.echr.coe.int/fre?i=001-236065.

## Conclusion

We began this Element by noting the relative scarcity of research on Jehovah's Witnesses, and while the bibliography indicates a modest increase of scholarship, we conclude by suggesting additional topics and approaches that would contribute to scholarly knowledge of this still-understudied community. We hope that our work helps to enhance the cultural literacy of researchers who will build on existing scholarship and move forward in new directions.

Public discourse on minority and new religious movements has long been disproportionately shaped by the critical voices of anticult and countercult groups, as well as by alienated former adherents. The current resurgence of anticult rhetoric, leveraging electronic media to extend its reach, threatens to perpetuate and amplify this imbalance. Until recently, many academic studies of Jehovah's Witnesses have been conducted from a Western perspective, where individualistic orientations and notions of personal autonomy predominate. Seen through this cultural lens, the consciously collectivist orientation of the Witness community has sometimes been interpreted as closed, cultic, or clannish. The dearth of culturally sensitive scholarship examining religious identity, personal commitment, and individual agency has tended to reinforce these views.

Recent scholarly contributions use a variety of disciplinary approaches to break new ground methodologically, topically, culturally, and geographically. Some researchers have strengthened their study designs by engaging with Jehovah's Witnesses at the local, regional, or headquarters level to facilitate access to study subjects, obtain historical documentation, or incorporate cultural insights into their questionnaires and interview protocols.

Several anthropological and sociological ethnographies have examined the lived experiences of Witnesses from fresh angles. Małgorzata Rajtar's (2016a; 2016b; 2018) study explored autonomy among Jehovah's Witness patients in relating to Hospital Liaison Committees and German health care providers. Anatolii Tokmantcev's 2023 PhD dissertation, "Jehovah's Witnesses in Post-Soviet Armenia," probed factors affecting the decision to affiliate with the Witness community against the backdrop of State and religious intolerance. Edward Graham-Hyde's 2023 PhD thesis "Empowerment & Conversion: A Contemporary Explanation for Why People Join Minority Religions" included active and inactive Witnesses and explicated "empowerment" as a mechanism impacting religious affiliation.

Three studies have considered the connection between Witness millennialist beliefs and their evangelizing: Justin Lee Haruyama's 2022 PhD dissertation "Mining for Coal and Souls: Modes of Relationality in Emerging

Chinese-Zambian Worlds"; Danny Cardoza's 2021 PhD thesis "Becoming Accountable: Jehovah's Witnesses and the Responsibilities of Evangelism," set in Bishkek, Kyrgyzstan; and Joseph Webster's thirty-month study of the millennialist expectations of Jehovah's Witnesses in Northern Ireland.

Regional studies provide examples of insights to be gained from quantitative and qualitative research. András Máté-Tóth and Márk Nemes' mixed methods study of Jehovah's Witnesses in Hungary includes an analysis of media reception, an online survey (n ≈ 9,000), and forty interviews with longtime Witnesses. Aldiyar Auyezbek and Serik Beissembayev's 2022 study "Views, Values, and Beliefs of Jehovah's Witnesses in the Republic of Kazakhstan" explored religious orientation, life satisfaction, family relationships, civil obligations, attitudes toward others (fellow believers, nonbelievers, former believers), and other social views. Abigail Ayiglo-Kuwornu of the University of Ghana Department of Teacher Education is leading a longitudinal mixed-methods study of the effectiveness of Jehovah's Witnesses' model of literacy in teaching young children to read in local languages and the model's potential applicability to the Ghana school system.

The 2023 study "Jehovah's Witnesses During and After the Genocide Against the Tutsi in Rwanda: Psychosocial Factors Related to Faith, Forgiveness, and Family" was conducted by the Organisation Religieuse des Témoins de Jéhovah du Rwanda and the World Headquarters of Jehovah's Witnesses. Valens Nkurikiyinka and Jolene Chu, principal and co-principal investigators, conducted a nationwide anonymous online survey in Rwanda (n ≈ 13,500) focused on genocide situations and other traumatic events, religious identity, psychosocial and prosocial attributes, group support, family satisfaction, and intergenerational communication. A 2024 study by independent Witness researchers Xiaojun Hu and Tadahiko Murata (n ≈ 7,000) examined Jehovah's Witnesses' views of their religion, family life, and physical and mental health.

Historian of American religions J. Gordon Melton is writing a history of African-American Jehovah's Witnesses spanning the late nineteenth century up to the present. Zoe Knox and Emily Baran, historians of religion and of Soviet Russia and the Soviet Union, respectively, are editing the book *Essays on Minority Religions and Religious Tolerance: The Jehovah's Witness Test* (in press), examining the critical role of Jehovah's Witnesses as a barometer for measuring the level of religious toleration and freedom in society. During 2024–2025, expert on law and religion Silvio Ferrari and sociologist of religion Siobhan McAndrew are leading a pioneering cross-cultural socio-legal study of Jehovah's Witnesses in six countries. The JW-MAP project seeks to compare Witnesses' religious motivations, attitudes, and practices with public perceptions in the context of the political and legal situation of the Witnesses in each country.

Future studies could link to broader research themes. For example, what do cross-cultural studies of Witnesses show about the formation of personal and collective religious identities? What are the processes of affiliation, disaffiliation, and reaffiliation for adult converts and those from multigenerational Witness families? How does religion shape attitudes and behaviors in conflict regions, refugee situations, or secularized cultures? What motivates individuals to belong to a marginalized religious minority, and how do they view themselves and others? What roles might Witnesses' publications in indigenous and sign languages play in mitigating feelings of stigmatization and isolation? What aspects of Witnesses' disaster preparedness and relief programs could be used to foster volunteerism and social engagement in other populations? Such research could be enriched by integration into mainstream research in such areas as health, communication, psychology, family relationships, moral and cognitive development, group processes, social capital, resilience, and growth – with practical implications for educators, social services, and healthcare providers.

We hope this discussion has helped to illuminate the rational processes and lived realities of becoming and being Jehovah's Witnesses – an individual identity built on a reciprocal, personal relationship with God, Jehovah, and a commitment to live for and bear witness to their Sovereign. We have described key structural and functional aspects of the Witnesses' worldwide organization and how Witnesses view their individual participation in communal religious activities as a contribution to the well-being of society as a whole.

Witness beliefs regarding the end of wickedness and the impending millennial peace are the pivot around which these expressions of faith revolve. Their future hopes govern the ways in which Witnesses carry out the Christian mandate to love their neighbors – by their ethic of nonviolence, their humanitarian efforts, and, most importantly, their evangelizing work – in the earnest conviction that God's Kingdom is the only lasting solution for human suffering.

In the face of mounting social, environmental, and political crises, such optimism may seem more idealistic than ever – but no less worthy of scholarly inquiry. Thus, concluding their 1997 article on Jehovah's Witnesses, Stark and Iannaccone voiced the hope that other scholars would "contribute to understanding a movement that is changing millions of lives" (155).

# References

## Watch Tower Society References

(WTBTS-NY – Watchtower Bible and Tract Society of New York;
WTBTS-PA – Watch Tower Bible and Tract Society of Pennsylvania)

Awake! (1984). "MEPS – An Exciting Leap Forward in Publishing." April 22. 21–7. https://wol.jw.org/en/wol/d/r1/lp-e/101984287.

(1986). "MEPS – What It Can and Cannot Do." March 8. 24–7. https://wol.jw.org/en/wol/d/r1/lp-e/101986170

Jehovah's Witnesses – Official Website (n.d.-a). "Medical Information for Clinicians." www.jw.org/en/medical-library/.

Jehovah's Witnesses – Official Website (n.d.-b). "What Is the Governing Body of Jehovah's Witnesses?" www.jw.org/en/jehovahs-witnesses/faq/governing-body-jw-helpers/

Jehovah's Witnesses – Official Website (2017). "Witnesses' New Branch Office in Britain Receives Top BREEAM Rating for Sustainable Design." www.jw.org/en/news/region/united-kingdom/branch-office-breeam-rating-sustainable-design/

NWT (New World Translation of the Holy Scriptures) (2013). "A4 The Divine Name in the Hebrew Scriptures." Wallkill, NY: WTBTS-NY, 1731–1735. www.jw.org/en/library/bible/study-bible/appendix-a/tetragrammaton-divine-name/.

NWT Online (n.d.). New World Translation of the Holy Scriptures (Study Edition) www.jw.org/en/library/bible/study-bible/books/

Russell, C. T. (1891). Thy Kingdom Come, Millennial Dawn. Vol. III. Allegheny, PA: Tower.

Watchtower (1879a). "Supplement to Zion's Watch Tower." July. 9–10.

(1879b). "'Do You Want 'Zion's Watch Tower?'" August. 2.

(1879c). "The Building of Zion." December. 3.

(1880a). "Write at Once." May. 2.

(1880b). "The Closing Work (No. 2)." July. 3–4.

(1881). "Anointed to Preach." July. 1–2.

(1882). "Questions and Answers." August. 2.

(1883). "A Harmonious View." April. 5–6.

(1889). "Protestants, Awake!" August. 3–5.

(1893). "Our Chicago Convention." September 1. 280–1.

(1894). "A Brief Sketch of the Development of Present Truth." April 25. 92–101.

(1899). "Views from the Watch Tower." April 15. 83–8.

(1903). "'Your Labor Is Not in Vain'" April 1. 106–11.

(1906). "'Truth Is Stranger Than Fiction.'" July 15. 211–27.

(1912). "Our European Conventions." October 1. 310–12.

(1917). "The History and Operations of Our Society." November 1. 327–30.

(1918). "Prominent Brethren Arrested." June 1. 171.

(1925). "Birth of the Nation." March 1. 67–74.

(1939). "Neutrality." November 1. 323–33.

(1959). "Questions from Readers." October 1. 607–8. https://wol.jw.org/en/wol/d/r1/lp-e/1959728

(1971). "Appointed Officers in the Theocratic Organization"; "A 'Body of Elders' with Rotating Chairmanship." November 15. 688–701. https://wol.jw.org/en/wol/d/r1/lp-e/1971843; https://wol.jw.org/en/wol/d/r1/lp-e/1971844

(1975a). "The End of 6,000 Years of Man-Rule Approaches – What Has Been Accomplished?" October 1. 579–81. https://wol.jw.org/en/wol/d/r1/lp-e/1975720

(1975b). "Question from Readers." March 15. 191–2. https://wol.jw.org/en/wol/d/r1/lp-e/1975210

(1976). "A Solid Basis for Confidence." July 15. 438–43. https://wol.jw.org/en/wol/d/r1/lp-e/1976525

(1980). "Choosing the Best Way of Life." March 15. 16–20. https://wol.jw.org/en/wol/d/r1/lp-e/1980207

(1996). "'Providing for One's Household' – Meeting the Challenge in Developing Lands." October 1. 19–31. https://wol.jw.org/en/wol/d/r1/lp-e/1996727

(2002). "Guide Your Steps by Godly Principles." April 15. 18–23. https://wol.jw.org/en/wol/d/r1/lp-e/2002284.

(2006). "'Let Us Compare Scripture with Scripture.'" August 15. 12–15. https://wol.jw.org/en/wol/d/r1/lp-e/2006603.

(2009a). "The New Birth – How Does It Take Place?" April 1. 8–9. https://wol.jw.org/en/wol/d/r1/lp-e/2009244.

(2009b). "The Apostolic Fathers – Truly Apostolic?" July 1. 27–9. https://wol.jw.org/en/wol/d/r1/lp-e/2009492.

(2010a). "Men, Do You Submit to Christ's Headship?" May 15. 8–12. https://wol.jw.org/en/wol/d/r1/lp-e/2010361.

(2010b). "The Apologists – Christian Defenders or Would-Be Philosophers?" June 1. 28–31. https://wol.jw.org/en/wol/d/r1/lp-e/2010411.

(2011a). "When Was Ancient Jerusalem Destroyed? – Part One: Why It Matters; What the Evidence Shows." November 1. 22–8. www.jw.org/

en/library/magazines/wp20111001/When-Was-Ancient-Jerusalem-Destroyed-Part-One/

(2011b). "When Was Ancient Jerusalem Destroyed? – Part Two: What the Clay Documents Really Show." October 1. 26–31. www.jw.org/en/library/magazines/wp20111101/When-Was-Ancient-Jerusalem-Destroyed-Part-Two/

(2012). "When Your Adolescent Questions Your Faith." February 1. 18–21. https://wol.jw.org/en/wol/d/r1/lp-e/2012088.

(2013a). "Feeding Many Through the Hands of a Few." July 15. 15–19. https://wol.jw.org/en/wol/d/r1/lp-e/2013532.

(2013b). "'Who Really Is the Faithful and Discreet Slave?'" July 15. 20–5. https://wol.jw.org/en/wol/d/r1/lp-e/2013533.

(2015a). "Build a Strong and Happy Marriage." January 15. 18–22. https://wol.jw.org/en/wol/d/r1/lp-e/2015042.

(2015b). "A Living Translation of God's Word"; "The 2013 Revision of the *New World Translation*." December 15. 9–17. https://wol.jw.org/en/wol/d/r1/lp-e/2015922; https://wol.jw.org/en/wol/d/r1/lp-e/2015923

(2016). "The Spirit Bears Witness with Our Spirit." January. 17–21. https://wol.jw.org/en/wol/d/r1/lp-e/2016045.

(2017a). "Who Is Leading God's People Today?" February. 23–8. https://wol.jw.org/en/wol/d/r1/lp-e/2017283.

(2017b). "Question from Readers." December. 16–17. https://wol.jw.org/en/wol/d/r1/lp-e/2017686

(2018a). "Baptism – A Requirement for Christians." March. 3–7. https://wol.jw.org/en/wol/d/r1/lp-e/2018322

(2018b). "Parents, Are You Helping Your Child Progress to Baptism?" March. 8–12. https://wol.jw.org/en/wol/d/r1/lp-e/2018321.

(2018c). "Let God's Laws and Principles Train Your Conscience." June. 16–20. https://wol.jw.org/en/wol/d/r1/lp-e/2018446.

(2019a). "Love and Justice in the Face of Wickedness." May. 8–13. https://wol.jw.org/en/wol/d/r1/lp-e/2019404.

(2019b). "Providing Comfort for Victims of Abuse." May. 14–20. https://wol.jw.org/en/wol/d/r1/lp-e/2019400.

(2021). "'The Head of Every Man Is the Christ'"; "'The Head of a Woman Is the Man'"; Understanding Headship in the Congregation." February. 2–19, https://wol.jw.org/en/wol/d/r1/lp-e/2021280; https://wol.jw.org/en/wol/d/r1/lp-e/2021281 https://wol.jw.org/en/wol/d/r1/lp-e/2021282.

(2022). "'Bringing the Many to Righteousness.'" September. 20–5. https://wol.jw.org/en/wol/d/r1/lp-e/2022568.

(2024a). "Trust in the Merciful 'Judge of All the Earth'!"; "What Do We Know about Jehovah's Future Judgments?" May. 2–13, https://wol.jw.org/en/wol/d/r1/lp-e/2024404 https://wol.jw.org/en/wol/d/r1/lp-e/2024405.

(2024b). "Jehovah Wants All to Repent." August. 8–13, https://wol.jw.org/en/wol/d/r1/lp-e/2024531

(2024c). "How the Congregation Reflects Jehovah's View of Sinners." August. 14–19, https://wol.jw.org/en/wol/d/r1/lp-e/2024532.

(2024d). "Responding to Sin With Love and Mercy." August. 20–5, https://wol.jw.org/en/wol/d/r1/lp-e/2024533.

(2024e). "Help for Those Who Are Removed From the Congregation." August. 26–31, https://wol.jw.org/en/wol/d/r1/lp-e/2024534.

Watchtower ONLINE LIBRARY. Study notes on 1 Timothy 5:8. https://www.jw.org/finder?wtlocale=E&pub=nwtsty&srctype=wol&bible=54000 5000&srcid=share.

WTBTS-PA (Watch Tower Bible and Tract Society of Pennsylvania) (n.d.). *Changing History, Unchanging Conscience: Deungdaesa Incident*. https://deungdaesa.org/en/.

(1896). *What Say the Scriptures About Hell?* Allegheny, PA: Watch Tower Bible and Tract Society.

(1959). *Jehovah's Witnesses in the Divine Purpose*. Brooklyn, NY: WTBTS-NY.

(1989a). "Abortion." In *Reasoning from the Scriptures*. Brooklyn, NY: WTBTS-NY.

(1989b). *Should You Believe in the Trinity?* Brooklyn, NY: WTBTS-NY.

(1993). *Jehovah's Witnesses Proclaimers of God's Kingdom*. Brooklyn, NY: WTBTS-NY. https://wol.jw.org/en/wol/publication/r1/lp-e/jv.

(1996). *The Secret of Family Happiness*. Brooklyn, NY: WTBTS-NY. https://wol.jw.org/en/wol/publication/r1/lp-e/fy.

(2018a). "Foreknowledge, Foreordination." In *Insight on the Scriptures*. Wallkill, NY: WTBTS-NY. Vol. 1, pp. 851–60. https://wol.jw.org/en/wol/d/r1/lp-e/1200001549

(2018b). "Soul." In *Insight on the Scriptures*. Wallkill, NY: WTBTS-NY. Vol. 2, pp. 1004–7. https://wol.jw.org/en/wol/d/r1/lp-e/1200004192.

(2018c). "World." In *Insight on the Scriptures*. Wallkill, NY: WTBTS-NY. Vol. 2, pp. 1205–10. https://wol.jw.org/en/wol/d/r1/lp-e/1200004627.

(2019). *Organized to Do Jehovah's Will*. Wallkill, NY: WTBTS-NY. https://wol.jw.org/en/wol/publication/r1/lp-e/od.

(2020). *Jehovah's Witnesses' Scripturally Based Position on Child Protection*. [online brochure] Wallkill, NY: Watchtower Bible and Tract Society of New York. www.jw.org/en/gov-resources/global-information-brochures/packet-jw-scripturally-based-position-child-protection/.

## Other References

Abrams, R. (1969). *Preachers Present Arms*. Eugene, OR: Wipf and Stock.

Afrobarometer (2023). Afrobarometer Data, Merged Round 8 Survey. www .afrobarometer.org

Aguirre, B. & Alston, J. (1980). "Organizational Change and Religious Commitment: Jehovah's Witnesses and Seventh-Day Adventists in Cuba, 1938–1965." *The Pacific Sociological Review*, 23(2), 171–97.

Ališauskienė, M. (2023). "The Othering and Resilience of Jehovah's Witnesses in Soviet and Contemporary Lithuania." *Numen*, 70(2–3), 163–83.

Althoff, F., Neb, H., Herrmann, E. et al. (2019). "Multimodal Patient Blood Management Program Based on a Three-Pillar Strategy: A Systematic Review and Meta-Analysis." *Annals of Surgery*, 269(5), 794–804.

Andersson, L. (2022). "'We are also just normal people, like everybody else.'" Master's thesis, Linköping University, Linköping, Sweden. www.diva-portal.org/smash/get/diva2:1708693/FULLTEXT01.pdf.

Armet, S. (2009). "Religious Socialization and Identity Formation of Adolescents in High Tension Religions." *Review of Religious Research*, 50(3), 277–97.

Artemyev, A. (2021). *Jehovah's Witnesses in Kazakhstan: Socio-historical and Theological Analysis*. Almaty: Artur Artemyev.

Auyezbek, A. & Beissembayev, S. (2023). *Views, Values and Beliefs of Jehovah's Witnesses in the Republic of Kazakhstan*. Study Report, Astana, Kazakhstan. https://paperlab.kz/.

Aydinli, A., Bender, M., Chasiotis, A., van De Vijver, F. J., Cemalcilar, Z., Chong, A. and Yue, X. (2016). A cross-cultural study of explicit and implicit motivation for long-term volunteering. *Nonprofit and Voluntary Sector Quarterly*, 45(2), pp. 375–96.

Balafas, S., Gagliano, V., Di Serio, C. et al. (2023). "Differential Impact of Transfusion Guidelines on Blood Transfusion Practices within a Health Network." *Scientific Reports* 13(1), 6264.

Baran, E. (2014). *Dissent on the Margins: How Soviet Jehovah's Witnesses Defied Communism and Live to Preach about It*. Oxford: Oxford University Press.

Barchas-Lichtenstein, J. (2014). "Jehovah's Witnesses, Endangered Languages, and the Globalized Textual Community." *Language & Communication*, 38 (September), 44–53.

Barker, E. (2023). "In the Shadow of Russia: Jehovah's Witnesses and Religious Freedom in Central Asia: Some Introductory Conclusions." *The Journal of CESNUR*, 7(1), 3–11.

Barnes, B. & Cherchi-Usai, P., eds. (Forthcoming). *The Photo-Drama of Creation*. Rochester, NY: George Eastman Museum.

Beaman, L. G. (2008). *Defining Harm: Religious Freedom and the Limits of the Law*. Vancouver: UBC Press.

Beckford, J. A. (1975). *The Trumpet of Prophecy*. New York: John Wiley & Sons.

Bengtson, V. (2013). *Families and Faith*. New York: Oxford University Press.

Besier, G. & Stoklosa, K. eds. (2016a). *Jehovah's Witnesses in Europe: Past and Present*, Volume I/1. Newcastle upon Tyne: Cambridge Scholars.

Besier, G. & Stoklosa, K. eds. (2016b). *Jehovah's Witnesses in Europe: Past and Present*, Volume I/2. Newcastle upon Tyne: Cambridge Scholars.

Besier, G. & Stoklosa, K. eds. (2018). *Jehovah's Witnesses in Europe: Past and Present*, Volume II. Newcastle upon Tyne: Cambridge Scholars.

Besier, G. & Stoklosa, K. eds. (2021). *Jehovah's Witnesses in Europe: Past and Present*, Volume III. Newcastle upon Tyne: Cambridge Scholars.

Bocci, P. (2019). "Planting the Seeds of the Future: Eschatological Environmentalism in the Time of the Anthropocene." *Religions*, 10(2), 125.

Bromley, D. ed. (1998). *The Politics of Religious Apostasy: The Role of Apostates in the Transformation of New Religious Movements*. Westport, CT: Praeger.

Bromley, D. ed. (2007). *Teaching New Religious Movements*. New York: Oxford University Press.

Cardoza, D. (2021). "Becoming Accountable: Jehovah's Witnesses and the Responsibilities of Evangelism." PhD thesis, University of Cambridge, Cambridge. www.repository.cam.ac.uk/handle/1810/336103.

Case, S. J. (1918). "The Premillennial Menace." *The Biblical World*, July, 52(1), 16–23.

Chaffee, Z. (1941). *Free Speech in the United States*. Cambridge, MA: Harvard University Press.

Cherniak, A., Mikulincer, M., Shaver, P. et al. (2021). "Attachment Theory and Religion." *Current Opinion in Psychology*, 40, 126–30.

Chryssides, G. (2016). *Jehovah's Witnesses: Continuity and Change*. Surrey: Ashgate.

Chryssides, G. (2022). *Jehovah's Witnesses: A New Introduction*. London: Bloomsbury Academic.

Chryssides, G. & Gregg, S. eds. (2019). *The Insider/Outsider Debate: New Perspectives in the Study of Religion*. Bristol: Equinox.

Chryssides, G. & Whitehead, A. eds. (2023). *Contested Concepts in the Study of Religion: A Critical Exploration*. London: Bloomsbury Academic.

Chu, J. (2015). "'No Creed but the Bible': The Belief System of Jehovah's Witnesses." *Religion – Staat – Gesellschaft*, 16(1/2), 109–46.

Chu, J. (2023). "When 'No Resident Will Say: "I Am Sick"': The Global Religious Response of Jehovah's Witnesses to the Covid-19 Pandemic." In G. Chryssides & D. Cohn-Sherbok, eds., *The Covid Pandemic and the World's Religions: Challenges and Responses*. London: Bloomsbury Academic, 185–92.

Chu, J. & Seminega, T. (2022). "Jehovah's Witnesses as 'Citizens of the Kingdom of God'." In S. Brown & S. Smith, eds., *The Routledge Handbook of Religion, Mass Atrocity, and Genocide*. New York: Routledge, 269–79.

Cohn, W. (1955). "Jehovah's Witnesses as a Proletarian Movement." *The America Scholar*, 24(3), 281–98.

Cornelissen, L. (2021). *Religiosity in Canada and its evolution from 1985 to 2019*. Insights on Canadian Society. Statistics Canada. (Release date: October 28, 2021). https://publications.gc.ca/site/eng/9.904476/publication.html

Côté, P. & Richardson, J. (2001). "Discipline Litigation, Vigilant Litigation, and Deformation: Dramatic Organization Change in Jehovah's Witnesses." *Journal for the Scientific Study of Religion*, 40(1), 11–25.

Czatt, M. (1933). "The International Bible Students: Jehovah's Witnesses." Essay. New Haven, CT: Yale University Press.

Di Marzio, R. (2020). "Being Jehovah's Witnesses: Living in the World without Being Part of It." *The Journal of CESNUR*, 4(6), 69–91.

Dirksen, H.-H. (1999). *Keine Gnade Den Feinden unserer Republik: Die Verfolgung der Zeugen Jehovas in der SBZ/DDR 1945–1990*. Berlin: Duncker & Humblot.

Dobbelaere, M. K. & Wilson, B. (1980). "Jehovah's Witnesses in a Catholic Country: A Survey of Nine Belgian Congregations." *Archives de sciences sociales des religions*, 50(1), 89–110.

Ellis, A. (1853). *Bible Vs. Tradition*. New York: Office of the *Bible Examiner*.

Ellison, C. (1991). "Religious Involvement and Subjective Well-Being." *Journal of Health and Social Behavior*, 32(1), 80–99.

ENDE CORPUS (2021). www.deitsch.eu/

Farmer, S., Gross, I., & Shander, A. (2023). *Blood Works: An Owner's Guide*. New York: City Point Press.

Fein, H. (1979). *Accounting for Genocide*. New York: The Free Press.

Fenelon, A. & Danielsen, S. (2016). "Leaving My Religion: Understanding the Relationship between Religious Disaffiliation, Health, and Well-Being." *Social Science Research*, 57, 49–62.

Foulkes, L., Leung, J., Fuhrmann, D. et al. (2018). "Age Differences in the Prosocial Influence Effect." *Developmental Science*, 21(6), e12666.

Furstenberg, F. F., Cook, T. D., Eccles, J. et al. (1999). *Managing to Make It: Urban Families and Adolescent Success*. Chicago, IL: University of Chicago Press.

Garbe, D. (2008). *Between Resistance & Martyrdom: Jehovah's Witnesses in the Third Reich*. D. Grimm, trans. Madison, WI: University of Wisconsin Press (original publication year 1993).

Graham, L. (2017). *Moral Injury: Restoring Wounded Souls*. Nashville, TN: Abingdon Press.

Graham-Hyde, E. (2023). "Empowerment & Conversion: A Contemporary Explanation for Why People Join Minority Religions," PhD thesis, University of Central Lancashire. https://clok.uclan.ac.uk/51529/.

Grandqvist, P. (2020). *Attachment in Religion and Spirituality: A Wider View*. New York: Guilford Press.

Greenhaw, L. H. & Koby, M. (2005). "Constitutional Conversations and New Religious Movements: A Comparative Case Study." *Vanderbilt Journal of Transnational Law*, 38(3), 615–78. https://scholarship.law.vanderbilt .edu/vjtl/vol38/iss3/1

Grew, H. (1855). *The Intermediate State*. Philadelphia, PA: H. L. Hastings.

GSS (General Social Survey) (2021). *2021 GSS (Cross-section Study). Documentation and Public Use File Codebook (Release 3b)*. National Opinion Research Center at University of Chicago. https://gss.norc.org/ Documents/codebook/GSS%202021%20Codebook.pdf

Haerpfer, C., Inglehart, R., Moreno, A., et al. eds. (2022). World Values Survey Trend File (1981–2022) Cross-National Data-Set. Madrid, Spain & Vienna, Austria: JD Systems Institute & WVSA Secretariat. Data File Version 3.0.0. www.worldvaluessurvey.org/WVSEVStrend.jsp.

Haldeman, I. (1915). *Two Men and Russellism*. New York: Charles C. Cook.

Hammer, O. & Swartz-Hammer, K. (2024). *New Religious Movements and Comparative Religion*. Elements in New Religious Movements. Cambridge: Cambridge University Press.

Haruyama, J. (2022). "Mining for Coal and Souls: Modes of Relationality in Emerging Chinese-Zambian Worlds." PhD thesis, University of California, Davis. https://escholarship.org/uc/item/7c37r79s.

Hendricks, J. J., Hardy, S. A., Taylor, E. M. et al. (2024). "Does Leaving Faith Mean Leaving Family? Longitudinal Associations between Religious Identification and Parent-Child Relationships across Adolescence and

Emerging Adulthood." *Journal for the Scientific Study of Religion*, 63(1), 23–41.

Hesse, H. ed. (2001). *Persecution and Resistance of Jehovah's Witnesses during the Nazi-Regime, 1933–1945*. Bremen: Ed. Temmen.

Hickman, J. & Webster, J. (In press). "Millenarianism." In J. Robbins & S. Coleman, eds., *The Oxford Handbook of the Anthropology of Religion*. Oxford: Oxford University Press.

Hivey, S., Pace, N., Garside, J., & Wolf, A. (2009). "Religious Practice, Blood Transfusion, and Major Medical Procedures." *Pediatric Anesthesia*, 19(10), 934–46.

Holden, A. (2002). *Jehovah's Witnesses: Portrait of a Contemporary Religious Movement*. London: Routledge.

How, W. G. & Brumley, P. (1999). "Human Rights, Evangelism, and Proselytism – A Perspective of Jehovah's Witnesses." In J. Witte, Jr. & R. C. Martin, eds., *Sharing the Book: Religious Perspectives on the Rights and Wrongs of Proselytism*. Maryknoll, NY: Orbis Books, 276–304.

Hu, X. & Murata, T. (2024). *Jehovah's Witnesses in Japan – A Quantitative Study: Summary Report*. www.jwj-qs.jp.

*Information on Conscientious Objection to Military Service Involving Jehovah's Witnesses* (n.d.). Office of General Counsel, World Headquarters of Jehovah's Witnesses. JehovahsWitnesses.pdf (ohchr.org).

Introvigne, M. (2024). "Jehovah's Witnesses and Shunning." *The Journal of CESNUR*, 8(1), 79–105.

Introvigne, M. & Richardson, J. T. (2023). "Why New Proposals to Criminalize Jehovah's Witnesses' 'Shunning' Are Wrong: A Response to Grendele, Flax, and Bapir-Tardy." *The Journal of CESNUR*, 7(6), 61–9.

ISSP Research Group (2020). *International Social Survey Programme: Religion IV – ISSP 2018*. GESIS Data Archive, Cologne. ZA7570 Data file Version 2.1.0. https://search.gesis.org/research_data/ZA7570? doi=10.4232/1.13629.

Kaplan, W. (1989). *State and Salvation*. Toronto: University of Toronto Press.

Knox, Z. (2017). "The History of the Jehovah's Witnesses: An Appraisal of Recent Scholarship." *Journal of Religious History*, 41(2), 251–60.

Knox, Z. (2018). *Jehovah's Witnesses and the Secular World*. London: Palgrave Macmillan.

Knox, Z. & Baran, E., eds. (In press). *Essays on Minority Religions and Religious Tolerance: The Jehovah's Witness Test*. New York: Bloomsbury Academic.

Korkiamäki, R. & O'Dare, C. (2021). "Intergenerational Friendship as a Conduit for Social Inclusion? Insights from the 'Book-Ends'." *Social Inclusion*, 9(4), 304–14.

Kosmin, B. & Keysar, A. (2009). *American Religious Identification Survey 2008: Summary Report March 2009*. Institute for the Study of Secularism in Society and Culture (ISSSC). 2. Trinity College Digital Repository. https://digitalrepository.trincoll.edu/isssc/2.

Lawson, R. & Xydias, G. K. (2020). "Reassessing the Size of Mormons, Adventists and Witnesses: Using Census Data to Test the Reliability of Membership Data and Accounting for the Disparate Patterns Found." *Review of Religious Research*, 62(3), 413–37.

Leahy, M., Hofmann, A., Towler, S. et al. (2017). "Improved Outcomes and Reduced Costs Associated with a Health-System-Wide Patient Blood Management Program: A Retrospective Observational Study in Four Major Adult Tertiary-Care Hospitals." *Transfusion*, 57(6), 1347–58.

Lehman, P. & Martinez, K. (2023). "Faith without Works?: Religious Salience, Pious Practices, and Adolescent Substance Use." *Crime & Delinquency*, 1–30.

Lofton, K. (2020). "Why Religion Is Hard for Historians (and How It Can Be Easier)." *Modern American History*, 3(1), 60–86.

Long, N. (1968). *Social Change and the Individual*. Manchester: Manchester University Press.

Luther, R. (2022). "What Happens to Those Who Exit Jehovah's Witnesses: An Investigation of the Impact of Shunning." *Pastoral Psychology*, 72, 105–20.

Macmillan, A. H. (1957). *Faith on the March*. Englewood Cliffs, NJ: Prentice Hall.

Mattei, L. (2023). "Jehovah's Witnesses and Bioethics, Right to Treatment and Religious Freedom." *BioLaw Journal (Rivista di BioDiritto)* (Special Issue 2/2023), 219–41. https://teseo.unitn.it/biolaw/article/view/2847/2686.

McAninch, W. S. (1987). "A Catalyst for the Evolution of Constitutional Law: Jehovah's Witnesses in the Supreme Court." *University of Cincinnati Law Review*, 55, 997–1077.

Melton, J. G. (2009). "Bible Student Groups." In J. Gordon Melton, ed., *Melton's Encyclopedia of American Religions*. 8th ed. Detroit, MI: Gale Division of Cengage Learning, 590–5.

Moorehead, W. (1910). "Millennial Dawn: A Counterfeit of Christianity." In R. A. Torrey, A.C. Dixon, & L. Meyer, eds., *The Fundamentals: A Testimony to the Truth*. Chicago, IL: Testimony. Vol. VII, 106–27.

Namini, S. & Murken, S. (2009). "Self-chosen Involvement in New Religious Movements (NRMs): Well-Being and Mental Health from a Longitudinal Perspective." *Mental Health, Religion & Culture*, 12(6), 561–85.

National Office for Child Safety (2021). *Jehovah's Witnesses 2021 Progress Report*. Australian Government. www.childsafety.gov.au/resources/jeho vahs-witnesses-2021-progress-report

Niebuhr, H. R. (1929). *The Social Sources of Denominationalism*. New York: H. Holt.

Nkurikiyinka, V. & Chu, J. (Forthcoming). *Jehovah's Witnesses during and after the Genocide against the Tutsi in Rwanda: Psychosocial factors related to faith, forgiveness, and family – Summary Report.*

Okun, M. & Kim, G. Y. (2016). "The Interplay of Frequency of Volunteering and Prosocial Motivation on Purpose in Life in Emerging Adults." *The Journal of Social Psychology*, 156(3), 328–33.

Olejarczyk, J. & Young, M. (2024). "Patient Rights and Ethics." In *Statpearls* [Internet]. Treasure Island, FL: StatPearls.

Ouily, H. J., Sabané, A., Birba, D. E. et al. (2024). "Neural Machine Translation for Mooré, a Low-Resource Language." HAL Id: hal-04425414, version 1. https://hal.science/hal-04425414.

Pachovskyy, Y. & Demkiv, O. (2019). "The Social Capital of the Community of Jehovah's Witnesses in Modern Ukraine: Sociological Discourse." *Academic Journal of Sociology*, 25(2), 25–33.

Paloutzian, R. & Park, C. eds. (2013). *Handbook of the Psychology of Religion and Spirituality* (2nd ed.). New York: Guilford Press.

Pargament, K. & Exline, J. (2022). *Working with Spiritual Struggles in Psychotherapy*. New York: Guilford Press.

Pargament, K. I. & Lomax, J. W. (2013). "Understanding and Addressing Religion among People with Mental Illness." *World Psychiatry: Official Journal of the World Psychiatric Association* (WPA), 12(1), 26–32.

Paxton, P., Reith, N., & Glanville, J. (2014). "Volunteering and the Dimensions of Religiosity: A Cross-National Analysis." *Review of Religious Research*, 56(4), 597–625.

Perkins, G. (2016). *Bible Student Conscientious Objectors in World War One – Britain: For the Sake of the Kingdom*. North Charleston, SC: CreateSpace Independent Publishing Platform.

Peters, S. F. (2000). *Judging Jehovah's Witnesses: Religious Persecution and the Dawn of the Rights Revolution*. Lawrence, KS: University Press of Kansas.

Pew Research Center (n.d.). "Views about homosexuality among Jehovah's Witnesses." *Religious Landscape Study*. Accessed April 26, 2024.

www.pewresearch.org/religion/religious-landscape-study/religious-trad
ition/jehovahs-witness/views-about-homosexuality/

Pohran, N. (2022). "Belief-Inclusive Research: Does Strategically 'Bracketing Out' a Researcher's (Religious) Beliefs and Doubts Limit Access to Ethnographic Data?" *Current Anthropology*, 63(6), 691–713.

Rajtar, M. (2016a). "Health Care Reform and Diagnosis Related Groups in Germany: The Mediating Role of Hospital Liaison Committees for Jehovah's Witnesses." *Social Science & Medicine*, 166, 57–65.

Rajtar, M. (2016b). "Jehovah's Witness Patients within the German Medical Landscape." *Anthropology & Medicine*, 23(2), 172–87.

Rajtar, M. (2018). "Relational Autonomy, Care, and Jehovah's Witnesses in Germany." *Bioethics* 32(3), 184–192. https://doi.org/10.1111/bioe.12424.

Ransom, H., Monk, R., & Heim, D. (2021). "Grieving the Living: The Social Death of Former Jehovah's Witnesses." *Journal of Religion and Health*, 61, 2458–80.

Resar, L. & Frank, S. (2014). "Bloodless Medicine: What to Do When You Can't Transfuse." *Hematology: American Society of Hematology: Education Program*, 1, 553–8.

Richardson, J. T. (1985). "The Active vs Passive Convert: Paradigm Conflict in Conversion/Recruitment Research." *Journal for the Scientific Study of Religion*, 24(2), 163–79.

Richardson, J. T. (2015). "In Defense of Religious Rights: Jehovah's Witness Legal Cases around the World." In S. J. Hunt, ed., *Handbook of Global Contemporary Christianity*. Leiden: Brill, 285–307.

Richardson, J. T. (2017). "Update on Jehovah's Witness Cases before the European Court of Human Rights: Implications of a Surprising Partnership." *Religion, State & Society*, 45(3–4), 232–48.

Richardson, J. T. (2020). "The Rights of the Jehovah's Witnesses in Russia and Beyond: The Role of the European Court of Human Rights." *The Journal of CESNUR*, 4(6), 58–68.

Rigal-Cellard, B. (2020). "An Introduction: Scapegoating the Jehovah's Witnesses to Maintain the Cohesion of National Communities." *The Journal of CESNUR*, 4(6), 3–10.

Ringnes, H., Demmrich, S., Hegstad, H. et al. (2019). "End Time and Emotions: Emotion Regulation Functions of Eschatological Expectations among Jehovah's Witnesses in Norway." *Journal of Empirical Theology*, 32, 105–37.

Rochford, E. B., Purvis, S., & Eastman, N. (1989). "New Religions, Mental Health, and Social Control." *Research in the Social Scientific Study of Religion*, 1, 57–82.

Rota, A. (2019). "Religion, Media, and Joint Commitment: Jehovah's Witnesses as a 'Plural Subject'." *Online – Heidelberg Journal of Religions on the Internet.* 14, 79–107.

Russell, C. T. (1876). "Gentile Times: When Do They End?" *The Bible Examiner.* Vol. XXI, No. 1, Whole No. 313, October.

Saliba, J. (2007). "Disciplinary Perspectives on New Religious Movements: Views from the Humanities and Social Sciences." In D. G. Bromley, ed., *Teaching New Religious Movements.* New York: Oxford University Press, 41–63.

Saroglou, V. (2011). "Believing, Bonding, Behaving, and Belonging: The Big Four Religious Dimensions and Cultural Variation." *Journal of Cross-Cultural Psychology,* 42(8), 1320–40.

Siewert, H. (2004). "The German Enquete Commission on Sects." In J. Richardson, ed., *Regulating Religion: Case Studies from around the Globe.* New York: Springer, 85–101.

Simard-Émond, A. (2023). "Understanding Conversion to Jehovism among Indigenous Peoples: The Case of the Kitigan Zibi Anishinabeg." *Social Compass,* 70(2), 283–303.

Smith, C. (2003). "Theorizing Religious Effects among American Adolescents." *Journal for the Scientific Study of Religion,* 42(1), 17–30.

Stark, R. & Iannaccone, L. (1997). "Why the Jehovah's Witnesses Grow *so* Rapidly: A Theoretical Application." *Journal of Contemporary Religion,* 12(2), 133–57.

Stone, L. & DeRose, L. (2021). "What Workism Is Doing to Parents." *Atlantic,* May 5. www.theatlantic.com/ideas/archive/2021/05/what-workism-doing-would-be-parents/618789/.

Storrs, G. (1855). *Six Sermons on the Inquiry – Is There Immortality in Sin and Suffering?* New York: Office of the *Bible Examiner.*

Streib, H., Hood, R., Keller, B. et al. (2009). *Deconversion: Qualitative and Quantitative Results from Cross-Cultural Research in Germany and the United States of America.* Göttengen: Vandenhoeck & Ruprecht GmbH.

Thoma, M. V., Goreis, A., Rohner, S. L. et al. (2023). "Characteristics of Health and Well-Being in Former Jehovah's Witnesses in Austria, Germany, and Switzerland." *Mental Health, Religion & Culture,* 26(7), 644–62.

Tokmantcev, A. (2023). "Jehovah's Witnesses in Post-Soviet Armenia." PhD thesis, University of California, Los Angeles. https://escholarship.org/uc/item/1jn618pr

Triandis, H. (1995). *Individualism & Collectivism.* Boulder, CO: Westview Press.

Troeltsch, E. (1931). *The Social Teaching of the Christian Churches*. New York: Macmillan. (O Wyon, translator).

USCIRF (United States Commission on International Religious Freedom) (2020). *The Global Persecution of Jehovah's Witnesses*. https://www.uscirf.gov/publication/issue-update-global-persecution-jehovahs-witnesses.

*Vine's Expository Dictionary of Old and New Testament Words* (1981). s.v. "Love." Grand Rapids, MI: Fleming H. Revell, pp. 20–2.

Wah, C. (2002). "Jehovah's Witnesses and the Empire of the Sun: A Clash of Faith and Religion during World War II." *Journal of Church and State*, 44(1), 45–72.

Wallis, R. (1976). Review of the *Trumpet of Prophecy: A Sociological Study of Jehovah's Witnesses*, by James Beckford. *The British Journal of Sociology*, 27(4), 522–3.

Wallis, R. (1984). *The Elementary Forms of the New Religious Life*. London: Routledge & Kegan Paul.

*Washington Post* (1918). "20 Years for Disloyal." June 22, p. 3.

Weiner, I. (2014). *Religion Out Loud: Religious Sound, Public Space, and American Pluralism*. New York: New York University Press.

WHO (World Health Organization) (2021). "The urgent need to implement patient blood management: Policy brief." October 19. www.who.int/publications/i/item/9789240035744

Wilson, B. (1973). "Jehovah's Witnesses in Kenya." *Journal of Religion in Africa*, 5(2), 128–49.

Wilson, B. (1977). "Aspects of Kinship and the Rise of Jehovah's Witnesses in Japan." *Social Compass*, 24(1), 97–120.

*World* (1914). "End of All Kingdoms in 1914." August 31: 4, 17.

Wright, S. A. (1998). "Exploring Factors That Shape the Apostate Role." In D. G. Bromley, ed., *The Politics of Religious Apostasy*. New York: Praeger, 95–114.

YouGov (2020). *YouGov Survey Results*. https://docs.cdn.yougov.com/o93kio300s/YG-Archive-11082020-TheosSpirituality.pdf

# Funding Statement

Funding from the Arnold-Liebster Foundation made it possible for this element to be published open access, making the digital version freely available for anyone to read and reuse under a Creative Commons licence.

# Cambridge Elements ≡

# New Religious Movements

## Founding Editor

### †James R. Lewis

*Wuhan University*

The late James R. Lewis was a Professor of Philosophy at Wuhan University, China. He was the author or co-author of 128 articles and reference book entries, and editor or co-editor of 50 books. He was also the general editor for the *Alternative Spirituality and Religion Review* and served as the associate editor for the *Journal of Religion and Violence*. His prolific publications include *The Cambridge Companion to Religion and Terrorism* (Cambridge University Press 2017) and *Falun Gong: Spiritual Warfare and Martyrdom* (Cambridge University Press 2018).

## Series Editor

### Rebecca Moore

*San Diego State University*

Rebecca Moore is Emerita Professor of Religious Studies at San Diego State University. She has written and edited numerous books and articles on Peoples Temple and the Jonestown tragedy. Publications include *Beyond Brainwashing: Perspectives on Cultic Violence* (Cambridge University Press 2018) and *Peoples Temple and Jonestown in the Twenty-First Century* (Cambridge University Press 2022). She is reviews editor for *Nova Religio*, the quarterly journal on new and emergent religions published by the University of Pennsylvania Press.

## About the Series

Elements in New Religious Movements go beyond cult stereotypes and popular prejudices to present new religions and their adherents in a scholarly and engaging manner. Case studies of individual groups, such as Transcendental Meditation and Scientology, provide in-depth consideration of some of the most well known, and controversial, groups. Thematic examinations of women, children, science, technology, and other topics focus on specific issues unique to these groups. Historical analyses locate new religions in specific religious, social, political, and cultural contexts. These examinations demonstrate why some groups exist in tension with the wider society and why others live peaceably in the mainstream. The series highlights the differences, as well as the similarities, within this great variety of religious expressions. To discuss contributing to this series please contact Professor Moore.

# Cambridge Elements ☰

## New Religious Movements

Printed in the United States
by Baker & Taylor Publisher Services